D5

SHARK FISHING IN BRITISH WATERS

(Previously published as *The Rubby-Dubby Trail*)

Born in 1939 in Valletta, Malta, and brought up in the West Country, Trevor Housby has travelled the world in his varying capacities as writer, photographer, guitarist, and angler extraordinary. More specifically, he has played a major role in developing new opportunities for shark fishing in British waters, by opening up hitherto untried areas and advocating the use of the sporting light-tackle technique.

A prolific author (nine fishing books to date and numerous contributions to the angling press), an acknowledged master of the art of making his own fishing tales come true, consultant to tourist boards and hordes of frustrated anglers – he is perhaps the most noted angler writing in this country today.

He attributes the fascination he feels for the giants of the sea – be they shark, whale, tuna or marlin – to an early love of such classics as *Moby Dick* and *The Old Man and the Sea*. His own latest book, *Big Fish*, is an account of his many battles with these sea giants.

GW00656049

Also available in this series

COARSE FISHING – Edited by Kenneth Mansfield
SEA ANGLING FOR BEGINNERS – Alan Young
CANAL FISHING – Kenneth Seaman
BOAT FISHING – Trevor Housby
STILL WATER FLY-FISHING – T. C. Ivens

Pan Anglers' Library

SHARK FISHING IN BRITISH WATERS

(Previously published as *The Rubby-Dubby Trail*)

TREVOR HOUSBY

UNABRIDGED

PAN BOOKS LTD : LONDON

First published 1972 as *The Rubby-Dubby Trail*
by Gentry Books Ltd
This edition published 1973 by Pan Books Ltd,
33 Tothill Street, London SW1

ISBN 0 330 23811 6

Made and printed in Great Britain by
Cox & Wyman Ltd, London, Reading and Fakenham

Contents

List of Illustrations

(between pages 72 and 73)

All photographs were taken by the author

Sharko!

It is eleven-thirty on a misty September morning. We aboard the *Silver Queen* are talking quietly and watching our shark-floats bobbing along thirty yards off the boat. Three miles inshore of us we can just make out the straight outline of Ventnor Pier and the hills of the Isle of Wight fading into indistinct shapes high above. For an hour we have drifted on a flat-calm, rather oily sea, and from the moment our tackle went over the side we have felt confident that today we will find shark. All the conditions are ideal for porbeagle, and on a day such as this we may well hit a bonus in the shape of a thresher shark. As is normal off this section of the Island, there is a noticeable absence of sea-birds, although when we arrived at the start of our easterly drift several high-diving gannets were working a mile off our port bow.

On this still, grey morning the mackerel are shoaling thickly on the surface and the slick of our rubby-dubby trail shows as an oily stain across the water. Directly in the path of this attractor trail and thirty feet beneath the surface, our double-mackerel baits hang suspended from partially inflated orange and blue party balloons. As the minutes tick by we continue to drift steadily on towards the distant Nab Tower, our expectations of a fish increasing with each passing second. At eleven minutes to one, a shower of panic-stricken mackerel break surface less than fifty yards behind our floats and we know with awful certainty that a shark has arrived, drawn to our boat by the invisible trail of our three-mile-long rubby-dubby slick. Once, twice, three times, the mackerel break surface, and each time they flurry our pulses quicken until the waiting strain is practically unbearable. Any second we expect to see one of our balloon-floats bob sharply and glide away out of sight, but strangely and unaccountably nothing happens.

After fifteen tense minutes we relax and begin to discuss the situation. Our skipper, Terry Floyd, is under the impression that the fish has by-passed our baits, gone under our boat and is now working away from us with the tide run. George Armit, on the other hand, believes that the shark is only small and has already eaten its fill of live mackerel which interest it far more than our double-mackerel baits which hang stiffly from the big hooks. Personally, I do not subscribe to either theory: from my own sharking instincts, sharpened by encounters with shark in many corners of the globe, I am fairly certain that the fish is trailing us silently, trying to make up its mind whether or not to take our carefully prepared baits. I have no direct evidence to support this theory but somehow I can smell shark, and this convinces me that the fish is lurking close to the boat.

At 1.45 exactly, the mackerel splatter across the surface once again, and within seconds a huge dorsal fin breaks surface, followed by a high crescent-shaped tail lobe. As the fish rises it turns to face the boat and rolls like a porpoise, exposing a vast back. As the ripples fall away we speculate wildly on its possible size, which is definitely greater than that of any porbeagle we have yet seen off the Island. The general feeling is that it could weigh in at anywhere between four and five hundred pounds. It is obviously a monstrous fish, but since porbeagle can be very deceptive in appearance we all tend to underestimate its weight.

Less than a minute after disappearing, it breaks surface again directly beneath my float, and then dives at speed, picking up the bait as it goes. The sudden jerk on the line is enough to snap the thread connecting the balloon to my reel-line, and as the free balloon drifts rapidly away I am far too busy feeding loose line off the reel-spool to watch its progress over the surface. Fifty-sixty-seventy-eighty-one-hundred yards of line rip off the reel, and still the fish shows no sign of slowing down to turn and swallow the bait. At one stage the line is running out so rapidly that it is no more than a blur between the heavy rod rings. Then, abruptly, it slows to a halt and as the heavy braided line slackens I feel that strange sickness which comes over every angler when he loses a really big fish.

For a half a minute the line between rod tip and water falls slack; then, gently, it begins to stir, sliding stealthily out, the limp coils straightening as the shark pulls out the loose line. Now comes the crucial moment of striking. Automatically, I put the big reel in gear, scan the line between the rod rings to make sure it is free to run out and brace myself for the strike. It seems to take forever for those last few inches of line to tighten, but at long last I can feel the movement of the fish through my rod tip. As the heavy rod pulls slowly down, I lean back and strike the hook home with a long, strong, upward sweep of the rod. Once, twice, three times, I strike, pausing only to reel up the slack line between each shoulder-jarring heave. Like most big shark this one is slow to wake up to the fact that it is in trouble, but on the third strike it gets the message loud and clear and storms off like a mad elephant. The sudden wrench on the rod pulls me off balance, slamming me hard up against the gunwales of the *Silver Queen*.

Nearly 400 feet away the fish is shaking its big head from side to side, and at the same time slapping its broad, hard tail against the heavy wire trace. For a moment or two it is content to fight in this way, but as I build up pressure it follows the pattern of most porbeagle and allows itself to be led back quietly towards the boat. With all but twenty yards of line back on the reel, I am waiting for the moment when it sights the boat. Still it advances and for the first time we all see it clearly – a monster of a fish, its huge pectoral fins outstretched like the wings of a great aeroplane and the white leech scars showing up plainly at the base of its pennant-like dorsal fin. It is a big one for sure, bigger in fact than any shark I have ever seen in British waters. Slowly it swims round the transom of the boat, perhaps five feet below the surface. Every detail of its great size can be seen clearly, even down to the slight movement of its massive gill slits.

Porbeagle of all sizes react in the same way during the initial stages of the fight and almost invariably it is possible to lead them up to the boat like a big dog on a lead. Then, suddenly their instincts take over and they are off and running, and from that moment on you have a fight on your hands. This fish is typical: as it swims past the transom, its tail breaks surface, lashing the water to foam and covering me in spray as it switches into top gear. This time there can be no doubt that the fish is alive to the situation, for the big reel screeches like a scalded cat as the shark tears off line. With over 150 yards of line out, the fish is still going strong. Although I am controlling the madly bucking rod without too much trouble, I am worried by the fact that at the most I had only a little over 300 yards of line on the reel to begin with, and as things stand at the moment over two-thirds of this is already out and trailing astern of the fish.

Floyd, like most good shark skippers, knows his fish and fishing and had started the boat's engine the moment the fish woke up to the fact that it was in danger. With the engine in reverse, I am now able to hold my own and even gain quite a lot of line. With this line back on the reel I feel more confident of the situation and begin to issue orders to the skipper. By putting the boat into forward gear and swinging her round in a half-circle, we are able to run up on the fish, gain a lot more line and so ease the strain on my arms and back muscles. At this point George tells me I have been into the fish for over twenty minutes and as yet it has not shown any sign of tiring. Even though I am resting as much as possible, I cannot afford to give the fish any respite: the more I make it work, the sooner it will begin to slow down.

Minute after hard minute tick by and with the sweat pouring off my face and body, and my back discovering entirely new dimensions in pain, I am acutely aware of the fact that I could weaken long before the fish; without a fighting chair to ease the pressure, my back, arms and legs have to bear the entire strain. Thirty minutes, forty minutes pass, then a whisper from George makes me realize that I have spent an hour on the fish. Terrible burning pains are shooting up my fore-arms and the base of my spine feels as though it has disintegrated – yet still the fish surges backwards and forwards past the boat. Then, when I feel I can stand no more, I sense a gradual weakening out there in the depths, nothing I can truly pinpoint but definitely something. It never ceases to amaze me how a new surge of strength and determination can flood through my body when, almost at the point of giving up on a fish, I suddenly realize that my own strength is beginning to tell on my opponent. From the second I feel this slight weakening, I begin to pile on pressure and the strain which has threatened to defeat me now becomes a pleasure to use.

This fish, big as it is, now becomes an obsession – at all costs I must get line back on the reel. Like a miser counting his money, I now gloat over each inch of line I gain. With pain, misery and absolute exhaustion forgotten, I forget about both time and the other occupants of the boat. At this moment there is only the shark and myself in the world and I want to kill this fish beyond all reason. As each individual yard of line builds up smoothly on the reel spool, I become more and more convinced that I still will ultimately win this trial of mind and brute strength. Records do not matter, this is just a personal contest between the fish and myself. A contest which only one of us can win.

After an hour and twenty minutes the shark is little more than a dead weight and with less than ten yards to go I know it is mine. Then, in a last flurry, the monster surges towards the boat, rolls over on the resulting slack in the line and is gone.

Just as quickly as that. One minute I am within a few seconds of a new British and possibly even a new world record fish, the next my rod is straight for the first time in nearly an hour and a half and I am left to contemplate a few feet of very frayed, stretched line which flutters weakly in the soft sea breeze. At moments like this it is impossible to realize that the fish of a lifetime has gone for all time, gone in all probability to die somewhere on the sea bed.

Less than an hour after losing this fish, I hooked a second which at the end of a half-hour battle came aboard without undue fuss. Later this fish pulled the scales round to just on two hundred pounds; a fine shark, but a small one in comparison to my big lost fish of earlier in the day.

The Poor Man's Monster

Shark Distribution in British Waters
Porbeagle Shark
Blue Shark
Mako Shark
Thresher Shark
Shark Attacks

Shark Distribution in British Waters

Shark of one sort or another can be caught at almost any point round the British Isles. Individual species, however, tend to be rather limited in range, although in most cases their feeding grounds overlap. This is particularly true in the south-west, where blue, mako, porbeagle and thresher shark all inhabit the same basic area. When discussing the range of each individual species, it is impossible to lay down hard and fast rules of any kind, as odd fish can and do occur in the most unexpected places. These instances are rare on the whole, but by no means impossible.

The porbeagle shark probably has the widest range of our four main species, occurring regularly all round Great Britain and Ireland. The bulk of the specimens caught come from areas located off the south and south-west coasts of England, and the south and west coasts of Ireland, but since these areas also happen to be some of the hardest fished waters in Europe it is scarcely surprising that they produce the most shark. Other areas which seldom if ever see an ordinary angler, let alone a dedicated shark man, could in fact be equally productive – they are simply never fished enough by anglers who have the necessary skill to locate and catch sharks.

A typical example of this is the famous porbeagle ground off the Isle of Wight. A few years ago, no shark angler worth his salt would have fished these grounds with confidence, yet since I wrote the first account of shark in Isle of Wight waters, many hundreds of very big shark have been taken. Anglers from all over Europe flock to ports like Lymington, Yarmouth, Keyhaven, Langstone and Portsmouth, specifically to try their fortune with the Island porbeagles, and very few of them ever go away without a big shark story to tell, or a batch of big fish photographs to show to their friends. On the strength of the shark it produces, the Isle of Wight area is at present the top porbeagle hot-spot yet discovered. However, I doubt if it is any way unique as a porbeagle holding ground, and I am quite convinced that in time many other equally good fishing grounds will be discovered.

Porbeagle hunting is a comparatively new branch of shark fishing, and it is only during the past five seasons that these particular shark have been caught in any quantity. Previously, most shark fishermen concentrated solely on blue shark, and porbeagles, threshers, and makos were all taken by accident on blue-shark bait. With the discovery of the Isle of Wight grounds, anglers began to realize that there were more porbeagle about than was originally thought and consequently became more inclined to try their luck with these fish. To their delight, they discovered top shark-fishing grounds in areas which were at one time thought to be completely devoid of shark. Typical examples are the North Devon coast, the Channel Islands, and even the English Channel off Newhaven in Sussex.

Some of the catches from these new-found sharking grounds have been extremely impressive. The present rod-caught record porbeagle came from the Channel Islands, and a catch of seventeen big porbeagle was brought in by a North Devon boat. So far, Newhaven has produced only smallish fish, but it can be only a matter of time before a big fish is hooked over these grounds. Consistent catches from these new-found areas are all that is required to encourage other anglers to experiment with sharking in hitherto untried areas, and I myself am quite convinced that there are few places on our coast-line which would not at some time or another yield porbeagle to any angler who was really willing to go out, day after day, in search of them.

Norwegian commercial fishermen employ huge long lines to catch porbeagle from both the Atlantic and the North Sea, and their consistent success with big shark in northern waters prove beyond a shadow of a doubt that Scotland and Northern Ireland hold immense opportunities for rod and line fishing. Even in the shallower areas of the North Sea, they have been long-lining vast quantities of porbeagle since as long ago as 1960, with the result that serious attempts are now being made to establish shark-fishing stations off the Yorkshire and Welsh coasts.

In Scotland, many attempts have been made to catch porbeagle on a sporting basis, although up to the time of writing only one specimen has yet been taken by fair angling methods. These results may well sound discouraging when compared to the quantity of shark so far caught in the south of England, but before dismissing northern waters as a waste of angling time one should remember that only two or three knowledgeable anglers have ever tried to catch shark off Scotland, whereas hundreds go sharking on an almost daily basis from southern ports.

A very similar situation occurs in Ireland, with most shark anglers fishing the south and west coasts, concentrating particularly on the Achill Island area and Galway Bay. Even before the last war, porbeagle were being taken in quantity around Achill Island, and anglers still head for this locality in preference to trying new grounds which have yet to prove their worth. Curiously, although Achill used to produce quantities of very big porbeagle during the early and mid thirties, the average size of shark now being caught tends to be somewhat disappointing.

I recently conducted a survey on the sea-fishing potential of Northern Ireland, paying particular attention to the Causeway coast. Although this survey was designed to cover all types of sea fish, I spent several days fishing the huge tide races of Rathlin Island in the hope of making contact with at least one shark. Geographically, the whole area around Rathlin Island is ideally suited to porbeagle, and as packs of these shark had been roaming the Donegal coast only a week before my visit, I had high hopes of success. In all, I spent two days drifting over all the most likely places, and only once did I get anywhere near hooking a shark. On this one bite, the shark (I can only presume that is what it was) pulled my balloon float sideways for several yards and then dropped the bait, failing to return. When I reeled in for a bait inspection, I found that one of my double-mackerel baits had vanished and the other was totally unmarked. Similar bites on the Isle of Wight grounds invariably came from smallish shark and I can only conclude that this is what was responsible for the one possible shark run I had in Northern Ireland.

Two months later, in September 1971, a local angler fishing an inter-club competition hooked a shark on the Causeway Bank grounds, which subsequently turned out to be a 47 lb porbeagle. This was a tiny fish in comparison to the huge shark we take in the south, but it was a porbeagle none the less, proving that my belief that shark could be caught from the ports of Northern Ireland was well founded. Since we consistently catch porbeagle of all sizes down in the south of England, ranging from 45 lb to four or five times this weight, it is quite possible that the next catch from Northern Ireland could weigh in at 200 lb or more. Thus, yet another porbeagle area has been discovered, as it is indisputable that where you find one shark, you will surely find others.

All in all, porbeagle have the most widespread distribution

of all common British sharks. Even more numerous but far less widespread in distribution is the blue shark, a fish which is caught annually in enormous quantities by anglers fishing from the south and north coasts of Cornwall and, to a lesser extent, those of Devon. Unlike porbeagle which at times come right inshore to feed, blue shark have a marked tendency to swim and feed well offshore. During June, they are usually at least fifteen to twenty miles out, but as the season progresses they gradually move in closer to land. Even then, they are rarely caught less than six or eight miles out, and they are usually found in deep water. Some big blue shark have been caught off the Welsh coast, and the grounds off the south coast of Ireland normally fish well for this particular species, although Irish blues seldom seem to attain any great size. Blue shark are essentially a warm-water species and, while odd specimens may occasionally occur in unlikely places, they generally confine their activities to areas where the warm Gulf Stream currents keep water temperatures fairly high.

The bulk of British-caught blue sharks are females. Occasional males are taken from time to time but this is the exception rather than the rule, whereas on the other side of the Atlantic, off the east coast of America, exactly the opposite situation occurs – male blues being caught in large numbers at about the same time as British anglers are hitting into the females. Marine biologists have come to the conclusion that the males and females meet somewhere in the Atlantic to mate, and then split up to go their separate ways for the remainder of the year. In the case of porbeagles, however, both sexes seem to mingle quite freely, and any large catch is likely to contain males and females in fairly equal proportions.

The mako is another warm-water shark which seldom ventures far from the Gulf Stream currents. Unlike the two species already mentioned, the mako is a moody, solitary hunter, leading a very nomadic existence and, to the best of my knowledge, seldom if ever hunting in a pack. I have heard of these shark being sighted off the Isle of Wight area, and even as far east as Littlehampton, but all my own shark records lead me to believe that they seldom work their way up Channel beyond, say, Start Point in Devon. In time, of course, it is possible that they will be caught right along the whole length of the Channel coast.

Looe, Mevagissey and Falmouth are the ports which bring in most of the rod- and line-caught mako shark and, with the exception of several outsize catches in the vicinity of the Eddystone Lighthouse, most of the recorded specimens have been struck over shark grounds west of the Lizard Point. Like porbeagle, mako have a definite liking for rocks and reefs, the Eddystone reef and Manacle rocks being typical examples. Presumably they hang around these areas picking up pollack and other rock fish, which provide them with an easy and readily available source of food. They also frequent typical blue shark areas, and I would say that as a general rule they prefer to live and feed well offshore.

Mako are great jumpers, and most of the anglers who have reported these shark off the Isle of Wight have based their reports on sightings of big shark clearing the water. Although this is typical mako behaviour, porbeagles, threshers and basking shark all jump on occasion, and since it is almost impossible to tell one big shark from another at any distance I doubt very, very much whether the fish seen are in fact makos. My guess is that they are porbeagle or small basking shark, both of which are very common visitors to the Isle of Wight grounds. I would be only too happy if some lucky angler proved me wrong on this point, but I have doubts whether anyone will ever catch a mako off the Island. In my opinion, mako hunting is a Cornish sport, and the further west you go, the more likely your chance of success. I have never heard of makos occurring off the north Cornish coast, nor for that matter off South Ireland, but both areas could in due course yield the odd specimen. At present, however, these shark are without question very limited in distribution.

P.T.

P.T.
Portrush

P.

P.

P.

Kilkeel
T.P.

Unknown

Unknown

B.P.T.M.

B.P.T.

T.P.

Rather unknown,
other than
fish caught
commercially.

P.B.T.

B.T.P.
Newquay

Weymouth
P.T.

Lymington
P.T.

Loog
Mevagissey
B.P.M.

M.P.B.

M. B.M.P.T.
P.B. Falmouth

Key
B. Blue Shark
M. Mako
P. Porbeagle
T. Thresher

Shark distribution
in British waters

Like the porbeagle, the thresher shark has a widespread distribution and can occur all round the British Isles.
Unfortunately, although not technically a rare species, very few
threshers are ever caught on rod and line, and thus few anglers
have had the opportunity to tangle with one of these grand fish.
Shark boats operating around the Isle of Wight, between the
Nab Tower, St Catherine's Point and the Needles Lighthouse,
probably bring in more thresher per season than the rest of the
country combined. Even so, I doubt whether more than six or
eight sizeable fish are caught in any one season, and the bulk of
these are accidental fish, caught on baits intended for porbeagle.

Commercial fishing records, however, show that net fishermen and long-liners regularly take threshers from Land's End
to John o' Groats, although most catches are made from Dover
down to Start Point. These shark also certainly occur in the
Bristol Channel and up round the Menai Strait, although
neither area is regularly fished by shark anglers. Specimens
weighing up to nearly 1,000 lb are thought to exist in British
waters, but as yet no angler has succeeded in boating one anywhere near this gigantic size.

Other far more exotic shark appear from time to time in
British waters. These rare visitors include hammerheads, six-
gilled shark, bramble shark, Greenland shark and even white
shark, known in Australian waters as the 'white death'. None of
these fish have to my knowledge been caught on rod and line by
British anglers fishing in home waters.

Porbeagle Shark

Far commoner than most anglers realize, the porbeagle shark
has a wide range of distribution which makes it catchable from
practically any point round the British Isles. Basically a cold-
water shark, the porbeagle can even be found off the north of
Scotland or Ireland in areas where other species of shark are far

less likely to occur. Couple this with the fact that it also tends to congregate fairly close to the shore, and you come up with a fish which can be caught by almost any angler from almost any point on the British coastline. Someone once dubbed the porbeagle 'the poor man's monster', a title which in many ways suits it well. Even shore anglers have caught big porbeagle on occasion, and the average boat angler, out for a day in the local fishing-club boat, stands practically as much chance of hitting one of these great fish as does the fanatical shark angler who

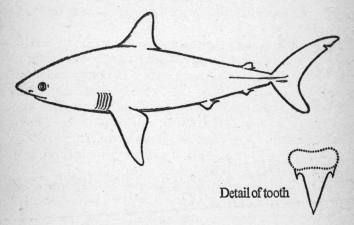

Detail of tooth

hires a proper shark boat for his day's fishing. Please do not think from this that I advocate shark hunting from small ill-equipped boats, for I do not, but I do believe that any angler using the right equipment stands a fair chance of contacting porbeagle no matter which port he sails from.

Like most sharks, porbeagle seem to have their likes and dislikes regarding territory. On occasion they can be found in the most unexpected places, but as a general rule they tend to live and feed close to tide races, reefs or rocky headlands, preferably when these are situated close to deep water into which the fish can retreat during periods of bad weather. Extremely catholic in taste, porbeagle will eat almost any fish it can find. Pouting, pollack, whiting, dogfish, mackerel, garfish, bream, small conger and various flatfish have also been found in the stomach contents of captured porbeagles, and at various times I have used most of these fish as bait with varying degrees of success. Weymouth boatman Tony Pearce has had several extremely interesting 'run-ins' with big porbeagle in the Weymouth area. On at least two occasions, anglers fishing from his boat have had hooked skate attacked by porbeagle. One shark in particular was so persistent that it took a 15 lb ray five times before finally tearing it apart at the side of the boat. Oddly enough, genuine shark fishermen have as yet met with only limited success whilst fishing the Weymouth area, although porbeagles, threshers and occasional blue shark are known to be fairly common in deep waters to the east and west of the Portland Bill tide race.

Porbeagles never seem to conform to a general pattern. Sometimes they swim and feed alone, sometimes in pairs, while at other times they hunt in huge packs consisting of anything up to thirty or more fish of varying sizes. These packs normally consist of small or medium-sized fish, but they sometimes contain the odd very big shark as well. Thus, one cannot assume that because several smallish fish have been caught one after the other there are no outsized specimens about. I have found that very big porbeagles often show themselves on the surface before diving down to take the bait. The sudden appearance of one of these monsters usually has a very bad effect on the novice or semi-experienced shark angler, which is one reason why so many huge sharks are lost during the first few minutes of the fight. I have known several extremely big porbeagles to be attended by one or more tiny shark, weighing at most 50–60 lb. These small fish usually take a back seat to the big one, but they occasionally pick up the bait before the monster gets to it. Nothing annoys me more than to see a really big shark idling on the surface close to my float, watch it go down and apparently pick up the bait, and then find myself firmly hooked into a diminutive shark which skitters about all over the surface, thoroughly alarming the big fish in the process.

In my experience, packs of porbeagle shark are encountered only once or twice in a season, but when the fish are found in quantity, sport can often be unbelievable. I have seen three fish hooked simultaneously – each successfully played out and gaffed without a line being tangled. During the time these fish were being fought, other shark could be seen lazing about just under the surface, while other more active fish made continual passes at the rubby-dubby bag. Having three fish caught together is a good start to any day's fishing, but to go on to catch nine more during the remainder of the day adds up to an unbelievable bout of shark catching, particularly when every fish caught was over the qualifying weight for the Shark Club. Quantity catches of quality fish are by no means common occurrences, but three to five good shark is quite a normal catch for the Isle of Wight grounds and more than enough to satisfy amateur and expert alike.

Big catches of heavy porbeagle shark have brought anglers flocking to the Isle of Wight area during the past few seasons, and I well remember being approached by a Dutchman during July of 1970 with a plea that he should come out with me to try to catch a shark big enough to gain him entry to the Shark Club of Great Britain. This gentleman had been to Looe for six successive seasons in search of a qualifying fish, but despite the fact that he had caught plenty of blue shark during each visit, not one had broken the 75 lb barrier. Now in desperation he was at Lymington, and having read of my successes, he came directly to me for help. This was on a Wednesday and it happened that the following day I was going out with local boatman, Jim Wreyford, and Graham Allen, a constant fishing companion of mine.

Jacob, our Dutch friend, was happy enough to join the party and as we steamed out to the shark grounds off St Catherine's, he could hardly wait to get his heavy and very expensive tackle together. Directly off Ventnor, we turned out to sea, put over our rubby-dubby bag and began a slow drift back along the edge of the deeps in the direction of St Catherine's Point. With a good, oily rubby slick out and a sea just ruffled by a fresh breeze, conditions seemed ideal. Within half an hour we saw our first sign of shark activity, as half a dozen mackerel splattered across the surface in obvious panic. Then, a hundred yards or so behind our balloon floats, a shark surfaced, wallowing gently through the tiny wavelets. The fish was obviously in no great hurry. It took its time approaching the floats, then directly behind my float suddenly burst into action and crash dived in a spray of white water. I was absolutely certain that this fish was after my bait but it was Graham's balloon that went crashing down. As the fish ran out slack line, Jacob and I hurriedly got our gear out of the way to give both angler and shark a clear field.

Graham was using a light boat rod and 50 lb BS line. Although we had all seen the shark and assessed it as medium-sized, it was obvious that he was going to have to play it carefully on the fairly light gear he was using. Throughout the forty-minute fight it was difficult to decide who was taking the most punishment. In my mind the Dutchman was, for from the word go he rushed about the deck like a madman, offering useless advice in a mixture of Dutch and perfect English. Finally Graham told him to shut up, and soon afterwards the fish was dragged over the side on the big gaff. Jacob had his bait in the water within seconds of the fish coming aboard. Obviously he hoped to get into a second shark before we could get our lines out. As it happened, he was unlucky, for this first fish was obviously a loner: we all got our tackle out again and drifted for well over an hour before the second shark struck.

This time Jacob was the lucky one and as his big 12-0 Senator started to screech out a warning, he slipped into his harness, settled his huge rod in a butt socket and sat back ready to strike.

Normally one waits for the fish to stop and turn the bait before attempting to set the hook, but this fish just ploughed ahead at tremendous speed without attempting to stop in the conventional manner, until finally our Dutch friend had to try to set the hook with the shark in full flight. A strike was out of the question so Jacob threw the reel into gear and leaned hard back as the full weight of the fish came up against the rod tip. So far so good. Obviously Jacob had caught enough blue shark to know how and when to set a hook, but he had never encountered a fish as strong as this one, whose sheer weight and brute strength came as a very sudden and nasty shock to him. He really believed at first that he was going to stop it dead in its tracks, but soon realized that the shark had other ideas. To give him his due, he settled back to fight it carefully, using the rod and the reel clutch as a true buffer against which the shark had to fight for its life.

For a while the battle surged backwards and forwards, neither side gaining or losing much line and both taking things fairly easy. Gradually, the spring of Jacob's big rod and the drag of his heavy braided line began to tell on the shark, and in typical porbeagle fashion it settled down after a while to a dogged, dour fight directly below the boat. Even an experienced big-fish man feels the strain of a prolonged battle, and Jacob, new to the catching of porbeagles, really began to take punishment as the fish surged back and forth below the boat. Then came a weakening on the part of the shark. The big rod had taken its toll at last, and the shark's strength was rapidly disappearing as Jacob strained and heaved on the rod.

Gradually the fish allowed itself to be pumped closer and closer to the surface, until it finally came into clear view, its white belly showing like a flag of total surrender. Inch by inch it came closer to Jim's mighty gaff and waiting tail-rope, and at last in a final flurry of blood and flying spray it was dragged bodily over the side. Somewhat bigger than Graham's earlier shark, this fish looked to weigh around 175 lb. Later we weighed it in at 180 lb on the quay at Lymington. Jacob's biggest-ever fish, and although we did not know it at the time, a new Netherlands record, which won him several cups and medals.

With two fish aboard and several hours' fishing still left to go, we all had hopes of some more sport. Shark were obviously on the move and with mackerel swarming round the boat and picking up bits and pieces from the rubby-dubby bag, we had every confidence in a third fish finding our baits. Suddenly and without any prior warning, my balloon went down and line began to melt off the big reel. The sharks were obviously ravenous, as both Jacob's run and mine were absolute scorchers. There was no point in giving my fish time to turn and swallow the bait since I was certain it had bolted it in its first strike, and so with line still roaring off the big reel spool, I threw the engaging lever over and hung on. The impact which followed practically pulled me off the engine box where I was sitting, and it says something for the Dacron line I was using that it could take such a sudden and vicious strain without parting. Fortunately, it held long enough for the clutch to come into full operation, and as the fish went into a crash dive I settled back on the engine box to give it as much stick as the tackle could take.

For thirty minutes it was solid give and take on both sides. Then the line slackened and I knew instinctively that the fish was coming up. Within seconds the shark hit surface and went over in a great porpoising roll. Almost immediately, it took on a new lease of life and went down at fantastic speed. Yard after long yard ripping off the wildly screaming reel marked its progress into the depths, until with a terrific crash it actually hit bottom. I had never known a shark do this before and I did not know just how to take this manoeuvre. I need not have worried: although I did not know it at the time, the fight was over. My fish was dead – its heart had burst in that last great power dive, its fighting spirit smashed by my tackle and the big shark hook.

Three hundred feet down, its lifeless body was just a dead weight on the line, and I had the job of lifting it, inch by inch, my back muscles screaming in agonized protest, my rod creaking as though it would snap at any second, and my mind filled with sick despair.

Time and again in the struggle to inch up the dead fish I cursed my luck and threatened to cut the corpse free, but I held on and finally my catch surfaced. Stone-dead, it rolled up in the trace wire, its heavy jaws sagging open, the rows of teeth glinting in the hot sunlight. Bigger than either of the other two fish, this shark later weighed in at 210 lb. I have never really known whether to be glad or sorry about this fish. I caught it fair and square, played it for over thirty minutes, and then had it die on me just when I had the better of it. I suppose I should be proud of it, but somewhere some of the glory rubbed off and even now I regret the way it came to the boat.

I think one of the joys of hunting for and catching porbeagles is that these fish live and feed close to the rocky headlands and violent tide races, where boiling overfall areas whip the water to foam even on calm days. Other shark tend to shun such areas. Even the mighty mako keeps mainly to the open sea, whereas the porbeagle hunts where the land- and sea-scapes are at their most dramatic. It is a grand feeling to fish big shark fairly close inshore, where a rugged coastline breaks up the monotony of looking at an endless vista of rolling water. Almost every real headland in the country holds a potential attraction for a marauding pack of hungry porbeagles, and many of the more likely areas are yet to be fished.

A group of Devon anglers, fishing off Hartland Point in North Devon, ran into a huge concentration of big porbeagles in an area where no one had suspected the presence of shark. Eighteen fish were hooked in a single afternoon, but only one was actually brought to the gaff; the rest were hooked and lost on tackle which just did not have enough strength to stand up to the big sharks. There have now been so many cases of anglers who, while boat-fishing for general bottom fish in close proximity to headlands and tidal races, find their baits being repeatedly snatched by hungry porbeagles, that it would seem that almost any headland which drops into deepish water can be a collecting point for this particular species of shark.

Porbeagles of all sizes venture very close to the shore on occasion, often into extremely shallow water. During the summer of 1971, a number of porbeagle were sighted off popular Hampshire bathing beaches and in several instances bathers were advised not to enter the water due to the presence of sharks. In Southern Ireland, one angler at least – Jack Shine – specializes in catching porbeagle shark from the shore, or to be exact from a rocky outcrop known as Green Island. Admittedly, the sea round Green Island reaches a considerable depth within easy casting range of the shore, but even so I do not think that this fishery is in any way unique. I can think of at least a dozen similar venues which could in all probability produce occasional sharks, should any angler take the trouble to fish them intelligently and consistently.

Jack Shine fishes very light, a 12-foot beachcaster, Alvey sidecast reel and 30–35 lb BS line being his standard tackle. From articles written by him, it would seem that the secret lies in having sufficient line on the reel to allow the running fish to travel three or four hundred yards at a time, and not in the actual strength of the line itself. A number of fish in excess of 100 lb have already been caught by this one angler, proving that shorecasting tackle can be perfectly effective in subduing shark, providing it is used intelligently and the fish is allowed enough line to run off as and when it feels the urge. I would very much like to try catching porbeagle in this way myself, and I hope one day to try and experiment along these lines from two Cornish headlands which look as though they might fish well in this respect.

Porbeagle shark can be very moody and I never know just how they will react from one day to another. They are frequently in a playful mood, and on the Isle of Wight grounds one can often see them playing with objects they find floating on the surface. Several times each season I encounter fish which show an interest in my balloon floats. They usually attempt to eat the balloon, and always seem surprised and puzzled when it goes off with a bang in their jaws. I can think of no good reason why any shark should attempt to bite a balloon, unless it somehow mistakes it for a sleeping sea-bird. This is a possibility, for on several occasions I have watched sharks, particularly blues, attempting to stalk gulls which have been resting on the waves. Presumably they have obtained easy meals this way in the past, but as yet I have never actually seen a shark catch a floating sea-bird.

Porbeagles that snatch at a float almost invariably turn down and take the bait, and it is a fairly general rule that any shark that shows on the surface can be induced to do this. Many fish show these same characteristics – splashing or rolling on top of the water as a prelude to feeding – and porbeagles are no exception. I like to see shark on the surface for it adds to the overall excitement of shark hunting, although to see a float suddenly disappear beneath the waves with no prior warning can also be tremendously exciting. Even so, watching a big fin or a fin and tail cruising straight up the rubby-dubby slick can be a heart-stopping experience, and only those anglers who have experienced this sort of thing will be able to realize just how the tension mounts as the big fish comes steadily onwards. Time and again I have seen sharks following a scent in this way, and when they finally reach the area of the balloon float even my nerves are jangling in anticipation of that final flurry of activity which will send them down to my bait, fathoms below the buoyant balloon.

Porbeagles of all sizes are strong, determined fighters, even if they do not battle it out in the spectacular and flashy style of mako and thresher. They are in all ways far superior to blues, which are poor fighters even at their best. On occasion, I have seen porbeagles turn on a tremendous turn of speed, often when least expected, and I well remember one instance of this. I was trying to gaff an apparently beaten porbeagle for a friend, when it put on such a dazzling last-ditch stand that it had us all doubting our ability to bring it to gaff for a second try at dragging it inboard.

This particular fish, which weighed only 120 lb, had a justifiable excuse for its sudden burst of energy, for in trying to gaff it in a really heavy swell, I had struck with the big flying gaff exactly when the boat began to surge up on the crest of a wave. The result was that, although the gaff engaged, the lifting boat combined with the sudden weight of the fish caused the gaff point to tear a ten-inch groove right across its flank. Until now, the fish had been wallowing on the surface, apparently beaten. The sudden gashing on its side, however, gave it an immediate and very violent new lease of life and it went off like an express train heading hard and fast for the bottom. The amazed angler could hardly believe the speed with which his line was disappearing, and all he could do was to stand there, trying feebly to apply the reel brake in an attempt to slow the shark down. It finally expended all of its energy, and allowed the angler to lead it back to the boat without further trouble. This time I got the gaff well in and the fish was ours.

This terrific turn of speed from an apparently beaten shark can catch any angler totally unawares, and as a result a great many good-sized fish have been lost at the very last moment of the battle. Because of this I advise all my shark-angling friends never to relax until the fish is right in the boat. Reel drags should always be loosened just before the gaff man goes to work, so that should the fish go raving mad at the gaff, it can take line off fairly freely without endangering the tackle. Anglers using centre pins should be even more careful, as the revolving handles of a big one can easily skin or smash a hand.

I have seen many big porbeagle off the Isle of Wight. Some

have been so enormous that at a conservative estimate I would put their weight at a minimum of 500 lb. These monsters seem to be more difficult to hook than the smaller fish, probably because they cannot be bothered to stir themselves for a small bait. Very occasionally, however, a really big porbeagle will snaffle a bait, and there are many stories of anglers, out from Lymington or Yarmouth, playing fish for two or three hours at a time, or being towed miles out to sea by fish which they never manage to see or to do anything with. Oddly enough, these outsized shark seem to lead a charmed life: time and again they are hooked, played and finally lost, for no apparent reason.

Blue Shark

My first shark, like the first shark of most sea anglers, was a blue — not big, not small, but just an average fish which weighed in at a fraction over 70 lb. The kind of shark which by my present standards I would return as quickly as possible to the water and say as little as possible about to my angling friends. In those far-off days, however, that shark came as the culmination of almost twelve months' hard work, and in terms of personal importance it was probably the most significant fish I have ever caught. Since its capture, my summer months have been dominated by sharks and shark fishing, both in this country and abroad.

As I have already said, that first shark was caught as a direct result of almost a year of planning. After driving down from London overnight, I arrived in Cornwall to find weather conditions stacked against me. I was booked to fish from a Mevagissey boat, and as I reached Pentewan Beach just outside Mevagissey, I could see that the bay was streaked with white horses driven up by a moderately strong easterly wind. I was brought up on this section of the coast and knew that few local boats ventured out in any sort of an easterly blow, and so with a sinking heart I drove on to hear the skipper's final verdict on the day. When I arrived at the inner harbour, the usual collection of blue-jerseyed trawler and long-line men were standing about swapping yarns and bemoaning the weather that kept them ashore.

Several sharking boats were laid up alongside the quay and as I walked over I could see that Albert Moorford, an old neighbour of mine, was aboard one. A typical, short, wiry Cornishman, Albert greeted me in traditional Cornish style: 'Hallo my handsome,' he said, 'you be along with me today, but I don't give much hope for a fish with this blast ol' easterly blowing.' Despite this prophecy of doom, Albert intended going out and as I took my tackle over to his big boat, the remainder of the party arrived. Cornish shark skippers almost always book individual passengers, and so apart from Albert I knew no one else on the boat. Typical of the average shark-fishing party, my companions were a pretty mixed bag – a honeymoon couple, a company director and his girl-friend, and a pale-faced lad who I knew instinctively would spend his day struck down with *mal-de-mer*.

After a quick check over the gear, Albert started the two big engines, cast off the bow and stern lines, and put the boat into gear. With the engines just ticking over, we nosed our way out of the inner harbour, past the lines of toshers and luggers swinging idly on their moorings. In comparison to the inner harbour with its crowd of boats and lack of room, the pool or outer harbour looked vast and empty, its sheltered waters calm and unruffled by the wind that blew outside in the open sea. As we slipped out through the harbour mouth under the shadow of the lighthouse quay, we slammed into a nasty little patch of wind-driven water before clearing away for Point Head. Once clear of the harbour Albert asked me to take the wheel, gave me a compass bearing to follow, and walked aft to mash up some putrid pilchard and mackerel for rubby-dubby. By the time we reached Point Head, he was back beside me giving directions and calling attention to the heavy white surf that smashed over the rocks below Chapel Point.

Beyond Point Head the loom of the Mighty Dodman made the barren Gwineas rock look tiny, although when we passed a quarter of a mile to the seaward side I could see that in fact it was quite large. Hundreds of cormorants sat on its highest ledges, holding their black ungainly wings out to dry, their crops full of fresh fish and their droppings staining the black rock white. Clear of the Dodman Head (once called Deadman for its reputation as a boat wrecker), we headed west towards the Lizard into increasingly bad weather. At a distance of approximately eleven miles from the nearest shoreline, Albert cut the engines, rigged the red mizen-sail to try to steady the boat, and then hung the rubby-dubby basket over the side to set up a thick oil slick while he put the tackle together.

By this stage I could hardly wait to get my hands on a rod, for although the boat was rolling like the proverbial pig, I was feeling quite happy. The young lad, however, was already adding his breakfast to the rubby-dubby slick, and it was fairly obvious from his general lack of colour that he was right out of the battle for the rest of the day. The honeymooners were in much the same condition but looked as though they would pull round should there be a chance of a fish. The outfits Albert produced were typically Cornish, although at that time, in my total ignorance of shark fishing, I regarded the short stiff rods, massive Fortuna reels and cord-like line as just the ticket. Pilchards were the chosen bait for the day – two big ones on each hook, suspended twenty feet below the surface by a couple of big crab-pot corks snicked on to the actual line. Once the floats were out, we in the boat settled down to await developments.

Naturally enough, having nothing better to do, we began to pay closer attention to the weather and soon realized that ever since the engines were stopped the strong easterly wind had increased considerably to nearly gale force. It had also begun to rain, and all in all conditions were becoming increasingly uncomfortable. It looked extremely doubtful that we would be able to continue fishing for very long. To make matters worse, our sea-sick friend was suffering very badly, for with no engine-power the big boat was wallowing nastily over the waves. The increased wind strength rapidly built up the size of the waves, and although we were in no immediate danger, conditions soon became appalling, with really huge, long seas the like of which one only sees off the Cornish coastline.

I suppose we must have flopped about for well over an hour before Albert decided on a bait inspection. To our chagrin, this showed both pilchards gone on one rod and just the heads left on the other. Obviously the sharks had found us, but as often happens in rough water, they had taken the baits without the floats showing any indication of a bite. For some time prior to this bait inspection, a dense shoal of big mackerel had been working on our rubby-dubby trail, and at Albert's instigation I used one of the boat's handlines to feather a dozen fresh baits. With a firm fresh bait on each hook, we all felt more confident of a strike. Sure enough, before the first bait had run back twenty yards, the float bobbed once and shot out of sight. At the same second, the big rod bent over and the reel gave a loud screech as the fish shot off just under the surface.

Being a sharking novice, I knew nothing of the finer points of shark angling. Consequently, I threw the reel out of gear more by instinct than by judgement and simply hurled myself into the fighting chair as the fish ran off, while Albert hastily strapped the harness over my shoulders and clipped it to a special ring whipped on to the rod. Throughout this operation, the fish had been taking line freely and I had made no attempt to set the hook. I must say that all my instincts were to strike at the running shark, but Albert had quietly told me what to do and knowing his reputation as a shark skipper I had controlled myself and followed all his instructions. Although the fish appeared to have run a terrific distance, only seconds had elapsed since it had taken the bait and I doubt very much whether it had run off more than fifty or sixty yards of line. Finally it slowed down and I could feel it pulling gently at the line. 'Hit it as it starts to move', Albert whispered in my ear, and I did just that. As the line began to move again, I tightened the drag, at the same time sweeping the rod hard back as the line came taut.

Looking back now, I realize that I hit that first shark of mine far too hard, but the heavy tackle I was using absorbed the terrific shock of my mighty strike and I knew for certain that the fish was well hooked. Typical of all blue shark, this fish made one reasonably hard run, slowed down to five or ten minutes of strong pulling, and then surfaced, rolled over twice on the trace and gave up the ghost. Albert's big gaff flashed once and in less than a minute the fish was inboard, its broad, beautifully shaped tail pounding away at the decking. There is nothing delicate about the average Cornish skipper's method of dealing with shark, and Albert was no exception. With half a dozen whacks of a seven-pound hammer, the shark was dispatched, ready for dumping into the fish hold.

When it first came out of the water, my fish was a beautiful, steely-blue colour, but as it died this faded to a drab grey. All sharks lose their colour in this way but none show it as much as the blue. All this had happened so very quickly that the fish was stowed away in the fish hold long before I had had the opportunity of studying it in detail. To Albert of course, shark catching was a daily ritual, but to me my first shark was something to be admired and savoured at length. With its rapid disappearance below decks, I felt somewhat robbed of my success and pleasure.

Our honeymooner was the next one away, and despite the fact that he was extremely sea-sick he struggled manfully into the fighting chair and harness, struck his fish, and with a grim face settled down to battle with the fish and his stomach. This second shark fought in a similar fashion to the one I had caught. This time, however, I had the opportunity to watch the battle as a spectator and not as a participant. Because of this, I was able to gain several clear views of the shark as it turned and twisted in clear water close to the boat. In its natural element, a blue is without doubt the most beautiful of all British sharks. Its superb colour and graceful shape give it a truly unreal appearance in the water, and I know of no other shark that, for sheer elegance, can match a big blue. This one fought for about the same length of time as my fish. The moment it came alongside, the big gaff came into play once again and within minutes it joined the earlier shark in the fish hold. Like all skippers, Albert lives on his reputation as a fish finder, and as each shark came in and was dealt with he ran up the traditional yellow pennant.

During the time it took to boat two blues, weather conditions had worsened, and with a very, very big sea running and the rain coming down in torrents, conditions were far from comfortable. The skipper's decision is always final and when Albert said pack up, that was that. He was obviously right, for we had the best part of fifteen miles to motor and for the entire trip the boat would have to punch on into a very heavy head sea. Cornish shark boats are usually built on the lines of the traditional tosher, with a forward dodger and open deck space, and Albert's boat was typical of its kind. This was just as well for us, as each sea we slammed into broke clear over the cabin and down on to the deck behind us. What with this and the steadily falling rain, our one-and-a-half-hour trip back to port was a far from comfortable experience. It was not until we rounded Point Head that the seas calmed down enough for us to go out on the main deck without being drenched by flying spray. During the final run in to the harbour, Albert dragged our two shark out of the fish hold and up on to the deck. I must say that I was profoundly shocked by their change in appearance, for up to that time I had not realized just how much colour loss a dead shark sustains.

With the boat tied alongside the quay, my first day's shark fishing was over except for the weighing ceremony. My shark in fact tipped the scale at 70 lb and the other at 5 lb less. Even in the steady rain, a crowd gathered to watch the fish hoisted up on to the scales. Although my shark looked bedraggled and very badly soiled by its confinement in the fish hold, I felt very proud indeed as I stood up beside it for a photograph. Despite filthy weather and extremely bad sea conditions, my first shark-fishing trip had, in my opinion, been a fantastic success. Later I realized that two medium-sized blues were a pretty poor return for a whole day's fishing, and as I loaded my tackle in the car, I made up my mind that I would learn as much as possible about shark fishing so that I could catch many, many more during future sessions.

I had to wait nearly a whole year for my next go at sharking. On this occasion I had three days' fishing booked at Looe, and in theory I knew just about all there was to know about blues. With the weather set fair, I arrived at Looe Quay on my first morning absolutely brimming over with confidence and anticipation. With my tackle aboard the lugger, I settled back to enjoy the trip out to the distant grounds. As we steamed out past the Banjo Quay, I could see that the open sea beyond Looe Island was as flat as a mill-pond. Away on the horizon a faint haze could be seen, whereas behind us over the land the air was crisp and clear. Early as it was, the sun carried a hint of warmth to come and I knew that we were in for one of those hot calm days which only Cornwall can produce.

One and a half hours out from port, we stopped for a few minutes' bait-fishing, and within seconds of dropping my feathers over the side, I caught a leash of six gleaming mackerel. After ten minutes of feverish activity, the bait box was full of frantically flapping fish, drumming out their lives in the hot sun. One hour later we were out on the ground several miles west of the Eddystone Lighthouse, on a sea as flat as glass, boiling with mackerel which dimpled the surface all round the boat. The rubby-dubby basket soon gathered thousands of mackerel round the boat, and it was obvious even to a novice like me that their feverish activity would attract any shark which happened to be cruising in the vicinity.

Only two of us were fishing on this particular day and with both sets of tackle out we settled back to watch the spectators haul string after string of mackerel into the boat. I have never been able to understand why people will pay to go out to watch shark fishing, when for very little extra money they could participate in the sport for themselves. None the less, Cornish shark-boat skippers make a lot of money from this spectator trade, and few boats go to sea without a full complement of onlookers who invariably shriek at the sight of each gaffed shark and expend roll after roll of film, most of which is out of focus or fogged by lack of photographic knowledge.

Less than ten minutes after the rubby-dubby basket splashed over the side, three fins came up about 150 yards behind our floats. Idling shark always appear to be lazy old fish and these three chaps were no exception, taking something like ten minutes to get up to our floats. To sit and watch three fins cutting slowly through the water within yards of your baited hook can be a nerve-racking experience, and by the time the first shark had completed his inspection and sunk from view I was actually shaking like a leaf. I knew that at any second the fish would hit one or other of the two baits and the anticipation of the strike had set my heart hammering so fast that I had difficulty in controlling my arms and legs. The interval between the disappearance of the fin and the first bite indication on the cork float could have only been a few seconds, but to me it seemed like hours. Strangely enough, however, the moment the float bobbed, my nerves settled down, leaving me with a feeling of utter confidence in my ability to hook and boat the fish.

High-summer shark are usually full of fat mackerel, and for this reason they tend to play with a bait for a long time before actually taking it into their jaws. This first fish was typical. It poked and pulled the bait all over the place without taking it properly, and for ten minutes or more the float dipped and dithered across the surface in the most infuriating fashion. Then, quite abruptly, the fish appeared to lose interest in the bait and the float stopped bobbing and floated serenely on the surface. I waited for several minutes, hoping the shark would come back, but nothing happened until I picked up the rod with the intention of inspecting the remains of my bait. Whether or not I moved the bait in picking up the rod, I shall never know, but as I straightened up, the cork float went down with an audible crack and yard after yard of line went whistling out through the rings.

Our skipper was a man who believed in leaving the angler to make his own decisions and it did not take me long to make mine. The fish was tearing out line and obviously had no intention of slowing down, so I did the only thing possible. I threw the reel in gear and at the first drag on the rod tip leaned back and hit the fish with everything I had. At this stage of my shark-fishing career I was quite convinced that all shark were really tough customers and had to be mastered from the beginning. This was unfortunate, for as I struck and heaved, the fish hit surface and turned over backwards. The impact of my strike and the shock of being turned over knocked all the fight out of it and within seconds it was alongside, ready for the gaff. That was it. My second shark was beaten before it even began to fight.

Naturally enough, this was something of an anticlimax for

me and for a while I was really disappointed that a biggish fish, with a fearsome reputation like a shark, should capitulate at the first hard pull. I realized later that in fact most medium-sized blues can be skuldragged into a boat on heavy tackle, but on this my second day's sharking, the lack of fight was a terrific let-down. Fortunately, although I did not know it at the time, we were in for a truly fantastic day's fishing – a day in fact which for sheer quantity of shark I have never been able to repeat.

Things went quietly after this first flurry of excitement and for another hour or so we drifted gently on over a sea as flat as tarmac. Then, without any warning, shark came up all round the boat, a veritable armada of shark, with fins everywhere and mackerel leaping in panic all around us. Both floats went down at the same time and both of us struck fish. Two anglers fighting two shark simultaneously from the same boat are in grave danger of losing one or both fish, as shark are notorious line-crossers and once two biggish fish become entangled a break is almost inevitable. Fortunately, on this occasion both sharks fought in different ways. Mine simply went deep and slugged it out directly below the boat, whereas the other angler's fish shot off across the surface and fought it out on a long line.

Mine was the first in the boat – a beautiful sixty-pounder. which quickly joined my other fish below decks. Less than two minutes after this was stowed away, the other one was on the gaff. Bigger than mine, this one looked a good seventy-five-pounder, and seemed almost certain to qualify its captor for membership of the Shark Club. The water round the boat was still alive with shark, and they took any bait we cared to drop in to them. Gradually, as the afternoon wore on, the fish hold filled up and in the end we had fish stacked all over the deck directly behind the fighting chair. The final count was eighteen fish, ranging from 45 lb to roughly 80 lb in weight; every one a blue and every one in fine condition. Eventually, of course, the remaining fish moved off, leaving us to tidy up the boat and make plans for the return trip.

I had already taken my tackle in when my companion's float went slowly down. 'Big shark', the skipper said, and I for one believed him. All the fish we had hit so far had pulled the float about for some time before dragging it down, but this last strike was different – no preliminary bobbings of the float, no ditherings on the surface, just straight down and away. There was nothing fast about this fish, the reel just kept turning gently as the line slithered slowly out. Later on in my career as a shark fisherman, I learned to recognize these symptoms and diagnose them as those of a big, unhurried fish. Even despite my total lack of big-shark experience at this time, I sensed something awesome about the slow deliberate way the big reel silently revolved as the line crept out and away from the boat.

By the time a hundred yards of line had gone, it was obvious that the fish on the other end had no intention of stopping to turn the bait, which was yet another sign that it was a big one. On the skipper's advice, my companion, now visibly shaking, threw the reel into gear, settled back in the fighting chair and, as the line on the surface tightened, struck the fish with everything he had got. Regaining the slack line, he struck twice more, and still the fish showed no sign of alarm. Slowly the thick rod bent over, and for a couple of tense seconds the straining angler held the fish back. Then, as is the way of big shark, the fish suddenly realized it was in danger and the reel began to purr and then scream as it started away.

We could see from the angle of the line that the fish was running close to the surface and we all strained to catch a glimpse of it, if and when it surfaced. We had the sun full in our faces when it finally came up, but it breached like a whale, rising straight up in the path of the sun and clearing the water by a good two feet. Details were impossible to see for the fish was no more than a silhouette, but it was big, very, very big indeed, looking to my inexperienced eye just like a big punt rearing up out of the water. 'Mako!' the skipper shouted, as it crashed back into the water with a belly flop you could have heard miles away. 'Mako and a really big one!' Twice more the shark shot up out of the water, and then turned and ran straight back at the boat. Winding like a maniac, the angler tried to keep up with the resulting slack, but the fish was travelling too fast, and as it shot past the transom of the boat it pulled out fresh line and came out of the water like a mad bucking horse. It seemed to me, as an onlooker, that the shark went higher than ever before, and at the peak of its jump I saw the big hook fly clear of its mouth.

Less than three minutes after it had been struck the fish was gone, leaving a boiling whirlpool of foamy water on the surface of a flat-calm sea and a multitude of memories which I doubt whether anyone on that boat will ever forget. It is impossible to estimate the weight of a big shark in the water, but that one was a monster. Between 400 and 600 lb was my guess, but no one will ever know for sure. At that time it would almost certainly have been a new British record, but you cannot claim for a lost fish.

Our mammoth catch of eighteen blue shark seemed poor compensation for the loss of the big one, but we cheered up on the long run back to port. By the time we steamed into the Looe River with a long string of yellow shark-flags flying, we were all back to normal and looking forward to the weigh-in at the quayside. If I remember rightly, only three of our catch of 'blues' qualified and as no one aboard the boat could remember who had caught what, neither of us entered fish to the Shark Club. Since this time, I have had many good catches of blue shark from both the south and north coasts of Cornwall and also from the west coast of Southern Ireland, but I have never managed to catch as many in a single day's fishing as I did on this second-ever shark trip.

Over the years I have caught several hundred blue shark and each one has convinced me increasingly that the only way to

catch this particular species is on tackle light enough to give the
fish a chance to put up some show of fight. My best blue shark
weighed 140 lb and unfortunately came on heavy hire tackle.
Thus, despite its fairly good weight, it did not put up a truly
worthwhile fight. A hundred-pound fish which I took on 35 lb
BS line and a very light boat rod, however, showed such a good
turn of speed that I was convinced I had hooked a smallish
porbeagle.

The drawback to light-tackle fishing is, of course, the chance
that you might well hook a shark of record-breaking proportions, and then lose it simply because the tackle has not got
enough strength. Personally, this is a risk which I am more than
prepared to take, for only once in all the times I have been out
after blues have I ever hooked a shark of another species. So,
with the odds at several hundred to one against hooking anything other than blues when I am out after this particular
species, I never mind taking the chance of hooking an extra big
mako, porbeagle or thresher and then losing it again due to
insufficient tackle strength. To be honest, however, I always
carry an assembled set of heavy gear, baited ready for instant
use should a big shark be spotted on the surface.

Mako Shark

In every part of the world where mako are known to exist, sport
fishermen rate them the gamest of all fighting sharks. Even in
British waters, where makos are comparatively rare catches,
anglers dream of hooking and boating one of these great game
fish just to become one of the rare few who have been fortunate
enough to add a mako to their list of captures. It was not until a
lady angler, Mrs Hetty Eathorne of Looe, caught a 352 lb mako
in 1955 that British shark anglers realized that it was in fact
possible for mako to exist in our waters; even this first specimen was brought in and claimed as a porbeagle until its teeth
were correctly identified in America. Since the first mako was

caught, an average of only four has been brought into Cornish ports each season, which gives some indication of the scarcity of this particular species in our seas.

The mako is very similar in outward appearance and fighting capabilities to a big porbeagle, and to the untrained eye it is very easy to confuse the two. Probably the easiest method of distinguishing one species from another is to examine the teeth. In the case of the mako, these are very irregular and rather long and rakish. Porbeagle teeth are much neater in outward appearance and each individual tooth carries two tiny cusps or tooth-like growths at its base. There is also a definite difference in the positioning of the dorsal fins, but this is difficult to ident-

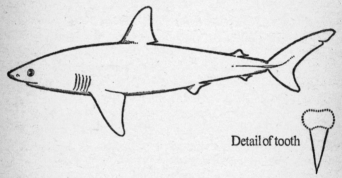

Detail of tooth

ify if you are not used to seeing both fish regularly. Another important difference is that the mako has only one caudal keel on each side of its tail, whereas the porbeagle has two. Perhaps the most distinctive feature of this shark is its habit of leaping clear of the water when hooked. Indeed, in New Zealand waters the mako is often called the leaping shark; a name which I think suits it well, since every mako I have ever hooked or seen hooked has cleared the water over and over again in its attempt to break free of the restraining line. Porbeagle rarely leap when hooked, although I have seen the occasional beagle breach.

Although, as I have said earlier, mako generally prefer to live and feed well offshore, there are definite exceptions to this rule. The most notable of these was the new record fish caught at the end of May 1971, which as well as being the first shark of the 1971 season was also the largest rod-caught shark ever taken in British waters. This huge fish was caught by Mrs Joyce Yallop, a sixty-one-year-old Norfolk grandmother fishing from the Looe boat, *Lady Betty*. Mrs Yallop had joined a party with the intention of going out after blue shark, for although the 1971 season had not actually started, several blues had been sighted by commercial boats some fifteen to twenty miles offshore. Just one hour after leaving harbour, the party sighted a huge dorsal fin projecting high above a flat-calm sea. Thinking the fish was a big basking shark, the skipper turned the boat to take the party up to it, intending to get close enough to take a few photographs before it sank from view.

It was not until the boat was practically alongside the fish that the skipper realized that it was not a basking shark but a mako, and a really big one at that. Oddly enough, it did not take much notice of the boat nor of its occupants. The boat's hire tackle was already made up but there was no fresh bait aboard, and so, rather than waste time trying to catch bait, the skipper decided to make do with a stale fish from the rubby-dubby basket. This stinking offering was dropped right in front of the great shark's nose, and, to everyone's surprise, the fish promptly swallowed it. Having given it plenty of time to get the bait and big hook well down, the lady angler set the hook and the battle was on. Although extremely sluggish when sighted, this particular mako behaved in typical fashion when Mrs Yallop struck the hook firmly home, fighting for two solid hours, leaping at least four times, and tearing out 300 yards or more of line each time it ran off. At one stage it even charged the boat, forcing the skipper to take avoiding action to save serious damage to his craft. When it was finally brought to the gaff, it had to be strapped to the side of the boat for the twelve-mile journey back to port.

How any woman could muster the strength to subdue a shark as big as this one, I shall never know, but beat it she did and in came a new record-breaker. Back at Looe, the fish was weighed in at exactly 500 lb, beating the previous record by a comfortable 1½ lb margin. This was an odd fish, caught in very odd circumstances. Firstly, it was hooked in May, quite close inshore, which is very early in the season for such a monster as mako are usually considered late-season fish. Secondly, it was hooked on a rotten mackerel, whereas mako normally prefer a live or freshly killed bait. And finally, when it was opened a recently swallowed conger eel, weighing exactly 50 lb, was found amongst its stomach contents. This really makes it stand out from any other mako which has ever been caught. The unexpected can happen at any time in angling, but to catch such a monster under these circumstances is so unlikely as to be almost unbelievable. However, the fish was caught and no doubt will stand as a record until a bigger mako is brought in to oust it.

I have brought several big mako to the boat when fishing off Portugal, but in British waters I have always been unlucky enough to lose any that I hook. The first mako I ever hooked off the Cornish coast was something of a revelation to me. Up to the time I hit this fish, my sharking experience had been limited to catching blue shark, whose feeble fighting ability had not prepared me in any way for the magnificent battle an angry mako can put up. I was back in Cornwall for an early autumn holiday and, having been down for a whole seven days, I had already had my fair share of blues, which to be honest were beginning to bore me a great deal. Then, quite out of the blue, came an invitation to go out for a night's commercial fishing; an invitation which I gladly accepted, particularly as the skipper suggested I brought some shark tackle just in case a shark turned up close to the nets.

We left the quay at about six o'clock and by the time we were out on the fishing grounds and had shot the long drift nets, it was well after dark. I felt we now stood little chance of contacting a shark, so I did not bother to put the gear out, although I had brought a handful of fresh mackerel along with me for bait. Around eleven o'clock a really beautiful moon came up, red gold in colour. Its pale light illuminated the oily calm sea all round the boat, showing clearly the position of the nets. A hot pasty and a tin mug of scalding coffee came up to me from the fug-filled galley and as I sat down to eat, my back against the wheelhouse, the old skipper came on deck to see if I was fishing.

I told him I had not bothered to put out a line as I thought we did not stand much chance of a shark. He, however, insisted I should at least give it a try. So more to humour the old boy than anything else, I slapped the hook through a couple of mackerel, measured off five fathoms of line, attached a couple of net corks as a float and dropped the bait into the dark clear water. As the two mackerel sank, a faint trail of phosphorescence marked their passage downwards until they were halted by the buoyancy of the corks. I let off roughly thirty yards of line, put the reel out of gear, and leaned the rod over the side of the transom while I finished off a second pasty and admired the colour of the autumn moon.

An hour passed uneventfully. Having no faith in shark catching at night, I began to doze off, expecting to wake only when it was time to haul the nets. At a rough estimate, I slept for half an hour, then woke with a start, for no definite reason. Somehow I could sense the presence of a shark close to the boat, although I shall never know why. Then, before I could climb to my feet, my big reel let out an angry snarl and the big rod pulled down as something dashed off with the bait. I could only think of blue shark at the time, but I knew before I touched the rod that if this was a blue it was a really big one. No small fish could have pulled off line as viciously as that. Naturally, as I picked up the rod I expected to feel the whole weight of the fish, but as I lifted it the line went slack. 'Blast!' . . . I thought, 'it's gone.'

Nothing further happened for several minutes and then I felt an almost imperceptible pull on the line. Big shark can sometimes be amazingly gentle and that tiny pull told me that my fish was still out there, mouthing at the bait. By slowly retrieving a little line I could feel more positive movements from the shark. Several sharp jerks told me that it had begun to gulp the bait down and I knew that at any second it would start to cruise away in search of more food. There was nothing further to be gained from giving it any additional slack line, so I put the reel in gear, waited until I felt the fish, then leaned hard back to set the hook. At this stage of the game, I was still expecting the fish to be a blue shark, and consequently was totally unprepared for what happened next.

Almost the second after I struck the fish, I felt the full power of it and realized that this was no blue. At the same time I felt the angle of the line change, warning me that the fish was going to come up, possibly to surface. In actual fact, the shark did a lot more than break water. It exploded out of the sea like a guided missile, stood up on its great tail directly in the path of the moonlight, and fell back with a splash which caused every crewman on the lugger to scramble up on deck in a state of semi-panic. Seconds after its initial leap, the shark was in the air again, rearing up like a mad horse in its effort to shake free of the hook. 'Christ,' said the skipper, 'look at that heller.' And heller it was, all twelve or fourteen feet of it – a real monster that reared and plunged in and out of the water until I felt certain my arms would drop off through strain. For nearly half an hour the fish kept just astern of the boat, leaping and diving, plunging and rolling. Then, quite suddenly, it settled down to fight it out deep down.

These new tactics were even worse than the aerobatics, as I had to keep maximum pressure on the shark to stop it running out all my line. This meant I had to stand up and fight it with every ounce of strength I could muster, my only support being the side of the wheelhouse which I used as a brace for my sagging back muscles. Time and again it ran off, tearing out line and each time I managed to turn it off course far enough to swing it round so that I could regain a little line. Finally, I had it back directly under the boat, crossing and recrossing, back and forth behind the transom. At this stage I really felt certain that the shark was mine. Both of us were weary but the fish had taken the worst of it and I was sure he was mine. I had known from its leaping ability that it was a mako, and now I felt confident of not only boating my first mako but also of smashing the existing record for the species, as this shark was far and away larger than anything that had yet been caught on rod and line from British waters.

They say pride comes before a fall, and my smug confidence in my ability to bring this huge fish to the gaff was suddenly shattered by a totally unexpected burst of energy on the part of my adversary. There was nothing spectacular about the way it ran off line. To begin with, I was more than sure that I could turn it in its tracks, and so I made the mistake of allowing it to pull off quite a lot. With over 100 yards out I suddenly realized that the fish had no intention of stopping. It was just determined to keep plodding on until either I ran out of line or it died in its attempt to escape. Nothing I could do made the slightest impression on its forward movement. It just swam on, totally ignoring heavy rod pressure. I could not even induce it to change course by laying the rod hard over to the right or left.

All through the battle I had been conscious only of myself and the shark. Now I suddenly remembered that somewhere out in the direction the shark was taking, a great wall of drift nets hung down in the dark water. Even as I thought about these nets I felt something grate along the line, and I knew for sure and for certain that my fish had hit and fouled them. To lend weight to this foreboding, the cork floats nearest the boat bobbed violently as something further along the net surfaced in a welter of white water and torn meshes. The skipper's language was unbelievable, and mine was not much much better when my line suddenly went slack. At first I hoped that maybe the fish had cleared itself and changed direction, but deep down I knew it had gone for good. How right I was. When I reeled in I found the end of my line frayed and ragged, and the trace, swivels and float gone, in all probability to follow the huge mako into the depths. The first drift net was also in pretty bad shape: a huge hole ripped in its meshes, a whole day's work required to repair it ready for the next night's work, and not a fish to show for its damage. Fortunately the others caught well that night, so the one torn and mangled net was not too serious. During the long steam home, the crew kept up a constant conversation about my lost shark. To a man, they all agreed they had never seen a fish like it, and as most of them had worked shark boats at one time or another they all knew their shark pretty well. In the following years, the old skipper, now unfortunately dead, often reminded me of this huge fish, and many a pint was drunk to its memory in the local pub or in the fisherman's club on the quay.

Mako are at best totally unpredictable fish. Nomadic to the extreme, they usually turn up when least expected and more often than not the angler who hooks one of these monsters promptly loses it again through lack of experience. I was out on a blue-shark trip from Mevagissey once when a completely inexperienced angler hooked a mako so large that it was almost difficult to believe that a fish of such colossal proportions could exist in British waters. The day in question was fairly good; a stiff south-westerly breeze put just enough chop on the water to make conditions pretty well perfect for sharking. We started our drift roughly ten miles out in an area which had been producing blue shark in quantity for several weeks and, naturally enough, everyone on board was expecting a good day's fishing.

Mackerel were extremely prolific, and it was only necessary to drop a leash of feathers down in front of the rubby-dubby basket to secure a full string of hefty Cornish baits. Each rod had a fresh fish neatly threaded on the hook and shark fever was rapidly rising amongst crew and passengers alike. For the first hour we all sat close to our tackle, each expecting a run with every second that passed. As time ticked on however, the lack of fish activity slowly began to take the edge off our confidence and general enthusiasm, until one by one we started to take full advantage of the warm sunshine and stretched out in the most comfortable places we could find. The skipper, worried by lack of shark bites, kept up a steady stream of invective, in between mouthfuls of hot tea and cake. Drifting can be a relaxing way of fishing if nothing in particular is happening, and by early afternoon half our complement of passengers were sound asleep and the other half, myself included, were well on the way to a similar condition.

The reflection of light against water made it virtually impossible to keep an eye on the cork floats, so apart from an occasional glance in their direction even I was content to drift without bothering my head too much about the fishing, or rather the lack of it. Suddenly, the reel on the rod next to mine gave a couple of anxious clicks. 'Drifting weed', I thought. Then, the big rod gave a heavy lurch and the huge Fortuna reel started to revolve at an unbelievable speed. Coil after coil of line leaped off the reel spool and actually whistled as it ran out through the rod rings. Fortunately the rod was tied down, otherwise I am sure the whole lot would have been jerked over the side as the fish ran off. Naturally enough, we were all taken completely by surprise at the unexpected abruptness of the 'take', and for several seconds pandemonium reigned as people rushed about trying to gather their scattered wits.

The skipper was as usual right on the job, untying the rod and handing it to the lucky angler, who by this time was seated firmly in the fighting chair, a look of nervous anticipation on his face. This whole operation took roughly ten seconds to accomplish, during which time at least 150 yards of heavy line had been torn off the reel. Obviously, the fish had no intention of stopping, so the angler had no choice other than to tighten up the star drag on the reel and set the hook. This brought an immediate and awe-inspiring reaction from the shark. The very second it felt the hook, it reared straight up out of the water, tail-walked across the surface for several yards, and fell back into the waves with an almighty crash. For several seconds there was absolute silence on the boat, then we all started to talk at once. This shark was not just big, it was enormous, a monster mako of unbelievable proportions. None of us aboard had ever seen anything to equal it in size in British waters, and yet somehow or other we had managed to get a hook into it.

The skipper and I both knew this one was a real record breaker, at the very least a 600-pounder, and its capture would give the skipper a big fish reputation which would earn him a comfortable living for many years to come – if and only if we could get it to the gaff and take it back for weighing. Within seconds of making its first leap, the monster was off and running again, dragging the poor angler hard up against his harness straps as he tried desperately to control the wildly bucking rod. Twice he tried to check or turn the big shark in its mad dash for freedom, and each time he applied additional pressure the shark came out of the water like a runaway steeple-chaser, its huge tail beating the surface to foam, streams of white water gushing from its broad underslung mouth. Each time it broke surface it looked bigger than ever and I began to wonder whether we had seriously underestimated its size.

With nearly 400 yards of line out, our skipper decided to try to run up on the fish, in order to allow the angler to get some badly needed line back on the big reel. This trick worked reasonably well to start with, enabling the angler to regain well over 200 yards of line in a few minutes. With this amount safely back on the reel, we kept the boat well away from the shark, advising the angler to give it as much stick as possible without straining the tackle too far. Fighting a big shark, particularly a mako, can be a long hard slog and it pays the angler to force the shark to strain against the elasticity of the rod rather than the actual muscles of the angler behind it. In this way the fish can be forced to wear down its own strength, while the angler conserves his for the final stage of the battle.

On this occasion, our angler was doing well. The rod held its battle curve against the pulling weight of the fish while the angler to some extent managed to take it easy. The huge fish had to be nursed as much as possible, however, for it was on a hair-spring at all times – too little rod pressure allowed it to get its head down, and too much brought it thrashing up out of the water to buck from wave to wave in a fit of aerobatic temper. This really was big-game fishing, of the sort we seldom see in British waters. Watching the antics of this shark made me realize just why anglers all over the world class the mako as the gamest living shark, a fish to be regarded in the same light as the mighty marlin, sailfish and tuna.

For an hour the angler hung on to the fiercely wagging rod, while the skipper performed complicated manoeuvres to hold the big boat close enough to the fish to keep it on a tight line and yet far enough away to avoid alarming it. During this hour we had worked several miles inshore and the high Cornish cliffs showed clearly. For a while a group of herring gulls wheeled round us, their heavy wings lifting on the thermals which spiralled them up high above our masthead, where they hung for long minutes before sweeping down to glide with effortless grace around our transom. Finally bored with the lack of activity on the boat, they made off shoreward, leaving us and the monster shark to battle it out in peace.

The strength of the fish was almost unbelievable. Time and again the angler tried to build up rod pressure, then in sudden defiance of the extra drag the huge fish would fling its mighty body skyward in a smooth effortless leap, leaving us breathless with fear lest it fall back on the steel trace or line and rip out the hook in its heavy jaw. I lost count of the number of jumps this shark made, and after the first hour no one bothered to keep track of time. Although we had all paid for the privilege of fishing, we realized that it might well take hours to break the fighting spirit of this great fish, and as one we were all more than prepared to sit back and forfeit our fishing time in the hope that the huge shark would finally become tired enough to gaff.

The angler was still in very good shape and for a novice he was handling his fish and tackle well. Quite suddenly, the shark tried a new trick. Instead of boring away from the boat, it turned and ran straight back towards us, the slack line hissing through the water as it came. Fortunately, the skipper was shrewd enough to anticipate this move, and by gunning the engine and turning the boat away from the running fish, he was able to keep it on a reasonably tight line. At the end of this run, the shark sounded, going down several hundred feet to sulk far below us. Again the heavy rod and line battled with the fish, and gradually, inch by inch, the spring of the rod lifted the shark upwards. This time the angler was forced to use pure muscle power to lift the fish and pump line back on to the reel. The whole operation seemed to take hours but, inch by inch, the line built up on the reel, until finally it was obvious to us all that the shark could not be far below.

Without warning, the trace swivel broke surface, and directly below it a long grey shadow suddenly appeared. At first the fish stayed down, a long sinuous indistinct blur. More pressure from the angler and it came right up, lashing the water to foam and striking the side of the boat half a dozen times with its mighty tail, before rolling once and moving off again. At first it swam slowly, then it gradually built up speed until once again the big reel was revolving in a blur of speed. The skipper, ever quick off the mark, was once again at the helm, both engines running flat out in an attempt to run up on the fish again. For several minutes it was stalemate, with neither side gaining or losing line. Then, almost imperceptibly, the fish began to surge ahead.

Time and again it porpoised over the waves, gaining yard after precious yard of line with every second.

We all had our eyes glued on the fish and none of us could understand why it should gain line so effortlessly. Finally, as one man, we turned to look at the angler, and to our horror found he had let go the reel handles and the lever brake. The fish was running free and wild and no attempt was being made to slow it down. Even as we watched, loose coils of line began to build up round the drum of the reel like some hideous bird's-nest. The end was obvious to us all, but the sudden crack of snapping line still caught us unawares, even though we had all been expecting it. Four hundred yards away, the shark cleared water for the last time. Up and up it went, shafts of sunlight reflecting from its wet skin, yards of loose line flapping loosely in the breeze, the long steel trace gleaming dully down its side.

As the skipper put the engines into neutral and walked aft, the silence was dreadful. All of us knew what was coming but none of us expected what would happen afterwards. 'Why the — hell did you give up?' said the skipper. 'I was tired,' said the novice, 'and anyway it was only a fish, so what's all the flap about?' Without another word, the skipper — beside himself with rage — punched the unfortunate angler firmly on the jaw, walked forward, put the engines in gear, and turned the boat for home. Unfair, maybe, but with a record fish practically beaten and his reputation at stake, I could not blame the skipper for his actions. Even I felt keen disappointment at the loss of this great shark. The unfortunate angler must have realized the enormity of his crime, for when we tied up at the quayside he did not make any fuss over the trouble. This was probably just as well, for the skipper was still seething about the loss of a fish which meant so much to him.

Ted Belston of Worthing is the only British angler to have caught two mako. Both were caught off the south coast of Cornwall, one being hooked off the Manacle Rocks, the other at a point directly off the Dodman Head. Ted told me that both fish were magnificent fighters and both were caught on days when other shark were noticeable by their absence. It is typical of a big mako to show up when least expected. They are so rare and elusive that no one can go out with the intention of taking a mako, although certain Cornish skippers do seem to be able to locate these huge fish should one be on the move. As yet, no one really knows anything about the habits of this species, but it would seem likely that a very big bait presented fairly close to the surface stands a better chance of attracting a mako than a medium-sized bait fished well down. Many of the huge mako which have been hooked have broken free simply because the gear being used cannot stand up to the strain imposed upon it by such a strong fish. The trouble is, of course, that using tackle heavy enough to subdue a mako spoils ninety per cent of the sport involved in catching blues and porbeagles. Thus, most shark anglers fish lighter and hope that, should a big mako turn up, they will have enough luck and line to beat it in a fair fight.

Thresher Shark

Only a very few lucky anglers have ever had the good fortune to hook and subsequently boat a thresher shark, and together with the mako this is a fish about which very little is known. In the section on shark distribution, I have mentioned that thresher have been reported from practically every part of the British Isles, although the bulk of these recorded specimens have concerned only stranded fish or fish caught by commercial fishermen. To date, rod and line anglers have failed rather miserably in their attempts to catch these shark in consistent quantities, or for that matter to pinpoint areas which are known to hold fair stocks. Commercial fishing boats working round the Isle of Wight regularly sight large thresher shark on the surface, and it would seem from the number of reported sightings that they are far more common in this area than is generally supposed.

Large female threshers seem to use this particular area as a place to drop their young, for during June and July of most seasons quite a few immature thresher shark are caught on mackerel feathers by anglers fishing within a mile or so of the Needles Lighthouse. As these catches almost always coincide with the sighting of a few very big threshers, it is reasonable to suppose that these immature fish are the offsprings of the big shark seen on the surface. Unfortunately, most of the very small threshers which are caught are brought in for display on the quaysides. This is a pity, for a 20–30 lb thresher is only a few weeks old, and to destroy fish as young as this severely cuts down future stocks in a given area. The huge tail of a thresher naturally makes it an object of interest to the average angler, who in all probability has never before caught a shark of any kind, let alone one as curious as this. Consequently, the fish is knocked on the head and brought in to be shown to all and sundry, until finally its captor finds it is beginning to decompose and dumps it in the nearest dustbin.

During 1971, I saw at least five little thresher pups brought in, their normally beautiful bodies covered in blood and grime, making them look so pathetic in death that I found it hard to imagine what joy their captors found in displaying their remains in public. I only wish it were possible to impress on anglers just how much harm they do by killing immature shark, but I am afraid that most fishermen still believe that by destroying as many sharks as possible they are helping to conserve stocks of bottom fish. It is impossible to explain to such people that predatory fish, like shark, conger, and tope, perform a necessary and very essential function, killing off all weak or ailing fish and keeping down stocks of bottom fish so that surviving specimens can grow to a good size.

Without fish like shark to keep nature's balance, most bottom fish would suffer from a population explosion, which in time would result in starvation. This in turn would cause fish to become stunted through over-breeding and lack of food, and in the end the sea bed would be inundated with tiny bream, flatfish, and bass which would offer little or no sport to the rod and line angler. In all probability anglers will never be able to grasp this idea and the slaughter of immature shark will continue until individual species are finally driven to extinction.

Of all British sharks the thresher is the most distinctive, and I doubt very much whether any angler could ever fail to identify such a fish. The huge sweeping upper tail lobe, big eyes, and snub nose of this shark make it stand out from all other species. The name thresher is said to have come from the fish's habit of thrashing the surface with its tail, in an attempt to concentrate mackerel shoals into a tight, easily manageable ball. I do not know whether the big tail is used strictly for this purpose, but I do know that when any thresher surfaces close to a mackerel shoal it certainly uses its tail to churn the water into a lather of foam and flying spray. In the old days of open-boat whaling, the whalemen were convinced that big threshers used their huge tails to slap whales to death. They then obtained an easy meal from the dead carcass. I doubt this story very much indeed, but there may well have been a reasonable explanation for threshers pursuing whales.

Under no circumstances could thresher shark be classed as pack fish, although they do occasionally swim and feed in pairs, each fish helping to churn up the surface – presumably to drive food fish into a state of panic. It is interesting to note that I have yet to see any thresher lounging about on the surface. Every fish I have ever seen on top of the water has either been lashing hard with its tail or leaping clear of the water altogether. Most sharks bask on the surface at some time or another, but thresher only seem to come up in a burst of wild activity.

Threshers certainly grow to an enormous size in British waters and fish of 600–1,000 lb are known to exist off many parts of our coastline. This being the case, it is odd that at present the record stands as low as 280 lb. Several fish approaching this weight have been taken, but as yet nothing to top it has been boated, although some monstrous specimens have been hooked and subsequently lost – either through bad luck or more often than not through bad fishing. Several really huge thresher shark were hooked off the Isle of Wight during the 1970 sharking season, but only one, a 201-pounder, was actually brought to the gaff.

Two Lymington anglers, John Roberts and the late Norman Baverstock, tangled with a monster thresher just a mile out from St Catherine's Lighthouse. On this particular day, I was out in another boat, and on a spur of the moment decision they decided to follow on in John's own boat, *Bunowen*. Both of them were experienced anglers, John in particular having a number of good porbeagle and blue shark to his credit. On arrival off St Catherine's, they found the tide just beginning to flood up toward the east. In order to avoid crossing our rubby-dubby trail, they decided to start their drift close inshore, with the intention of following the inshore edge of St Catherine's deeps. They had already feathered a few fresh mackerel on their way out and their shark tackle was made up and already baited when they cut *Bunowen*'s engines.

John was the first to lower his tackle over the side, but as his balloon float came hard up against the rubber stop on his reel line, it went straight down instead of bobbing about gently on the surface. Thinking that in some inexplicable way his bait and trace were too heavy for the normally buoyant balloon to support, John slipped the reel in gear and tried to wind in his tackle. Before the reel spool had turned once, however, he felt a tremendous snatch at the rod tip and realized that a shark had taken the bait as it sank down below the boat. More by instinct than intention, he automatically struck hard at the pull of the fish, and then sat back in amazement as a mighty shark leaped clear of the water right beside the boat. As the fish hit the water the big Tatler reel burst into a hoarse purr which quickly changed into a frantic scream, as the shark went off like a mad thing. One hundred yards out it surfaced again and cleared the water for the second time, its huge tail lifting high and clear for both anglers to see.

Both John and Norman now realized for the first time that the fish was a thresher, and no medium-sized fish at that. Yards of line vanished off the wildly turning reel, and although John tried every trick in the book in a desperate attempt to turn the fish, the shark just kept on steaming away at an almost unbelievable speed. By this stage Norman had the engine running, and to try to gain line they made a desperate attempt to run up on the shark. For ten minutes or more they chased the great fish. Then, almost imperceptibly, John began to get line back on the reel, an inch here, a foot there – nothing to crow about but enough to raise their hopes as the line began to build steadily up on the reel drum. Twenty minutes of this and the huge fish went down deep to sulk. With the boat out of gear, John settled down to the back-breaking task of raising the fish by pumping the heavy rod up and down.

For a while it was stalemate, the fish being strong enough to hold its position despite every effort John made to try to force it up. Then, suddenly, it began to give, and the taut line fell slack as the fish came up at unexpected speed. To try to keep a tight line on it, John wound the handles of the big Tatler reel as fast as he could, for he knew that if the fish hit surface and breached to fall back on the slack line, a break would be almost a certainty. Fortunately, the fish changed its angle of climb, and this was without doubt the only thing which saved the line.

This was John's first encounter of any sort with a thresher, and although he had heard of them jumping repeatedly when hooked all the wild stories still did not prepare him for the display of aerobatic fireworks which the shark put on. Time and again it lunged out of the water, giving the two anglers a clear view of its entire body as it jumped. Norman told me that he counted eleven jumps in less than four minutes. Each time it surged upwards, the two anglers waited with baited breath for the hook to shake free of its jaw, or for its heavy body to crash down on the line. Each time their luck held out, until the mighty fish disappeared again into the depths, its great scythe-like tail flailing the surface water to foam as it plunged down-wards. John's confidence in his ability to beat this monster now gave him the extra strength to force the pace, and the shark, obviously tired from its aerial exertions, grudgingly slowed to a halt, turned slowly in a tight half-circle, and began to give line again. Well over forty minutes had now passed and the fish was obviously very tired indeed. Suddenly, it surfaced, rolled slowly over and went down again, taking less than five yards of line before stopping to shake its head wearily at the agony of the steel in its jaws.

Fully realizing that the end of the battle was near, John piled on pressure, his heavy rod bowing hard down as he forced the fish up. At this stage, Norman reached for the gaff and found to his absolute horror that although the flying gaff head was in its normal place, the long handle was missing. A hurried search of the boat showed the total absence of the handle, without which the wicked gaff head was as useless as a piece of soft wire. The thresher was right alongside the boat by this time and, as John stood up to look over the side, the huge tail lobe lashed along the gunnel within inches of his face. Time and again the shark flailed the side of the boat with its mighty tail, as Norman desperately tried to shave down a boat-hook handle to fit into the socket of the gaff head. The shark still continued to lash at the boat, but each second that it rested on the surface it regained its strength, and before Norman could finish hacking at the improvised handle the great shark turned down under the boat, taking foot after precious foot of line off the big reel as it dived slowly beneath the waves.

Trying desperately to check its downward surge, John felt the Terylene line grate against the keel of the boat. Then suddenly, his rod tip sprang back and a few feet of frayed line fluttered out of the water to blow up in the gentle offshore breeze. Somewhere below the boat a monster thresher sank slowly into the depths, its great tail wagging feebly, the long steel trace still dangling limply from its vast jaws. On the boat both John and Norman slumped back in total disbelief. A few seconds earlier both were confident of boating a record-breaker, and now, thanks to the unknown vandal who had stolen the essential gaff handle from the boat, a record-breaking fish was lost for ever. How big that particular thresher was, no one can ever say, but both Norman and John gave a conservative estimate of 300 lb plus, and Norman – who tragically drowned at sea only a few short weeks afterwards – told me that in his opinion the shark was 12–14 feet in length, from its head to the tip of its tail.

In comparison to this fish, my own modest thresher was something of a huge anti-climax. Even so, I am still one of the few British anglers to have successfully hooked and beaten a thresher shark over the qualifying weight, and because of this and the splendid fight the fish put up I feel that it warrants a mention in this book. I hooked it during mid-August 1971, at a time when shark fishing is notoriously poor off the Isle of Wight. On the day in question I was out as guest and general shark finder with a party of semi-experienced shark anglers, who had yet to boat a fish from the Isle of Wight grounds. We started our drift just short of Dunose Head and east of Ventnor Pier, the ebb tide setting us directly down through St Catherine's deeps. Before starting, we ran a fair way out as a boat with a television crew was already drifting fairly close inshore and we did not want to spoil their rubby-dubby trail by starting operations too close to their position.

As a guest, I made sure that the other two anglers' baits and gear were out and settled before I attempted to set up my own tackle ready for use. I suppose we had been on the drift for only ten minutes at the most before I swung my double frozen mackerel bait over the side. As the float slithered up to the rubber line stop, I paid off slack line and trotted the bait out towards the two balloons already in the water. At the exact moment that my float reached the other two, it went down with a wallop which set the reel spool spinning. My two friends promptly pulled their own gear in, leaving me a clear field to play with the shark which had taken my bait. I knew from the start that this was not a porbeagle – the bite was far too decisive. As the fish turned and swam back behind the boat, I decided to take a chance on striking while it was practically under the rod tip. Normally, I would have delayed my strike to give the fish time to turn and swallow the bait, but as my balloon had not re-appeared on the surface I felt confident that the shark had bolted the twin mackerel, hook and all, within seconds of snatching the float down out of sight.

By this time, I had all the slack line back on the reel. At the first impression of movement on the other end of the taut line, I slammed the rod hard back over my shoulder, with the full intention of winding in the resulting slack and hitting the fish again to make sure the hook was firmly embedded. I never had time to attempt a second strike, for as soon as the fish felt the hook the big reel let out a high pitched scream, leaving me to gape stupidly at a fast emptying reel spool. No more than five seconds later, with nearly 300 yards of line out behind it, the shark hit surface twice, swept round in a great half-circle, and cleared the water astern of the boat like a champion steeple-chaser. It gave everyone in the boat a clear view of its neat body and high arching tail, as it bounded about over the surface like a rubber ball.

Within moments of going down, it was off again on another long tearing run which whipped line off the reel faster than any shark I have yet hooked in British waters. If I had not in fact seen the fish clearly, I could have easily mistaken it for a well-hooked tuna, one of the fastest moving fish I have ever caught. This was not shark fishing as I knew it. Any fish which could run out line this fast, then jump two or three times before doubling back on itself at full speed, was without question in the real game-fish class. No dour sulking down below the boat for this chap – it was fast action and airborne fireworks all the way, and with each jump it made my heart was in my mouth, waiting for a break to occur. Although I knew already that it was no more than 100 lb in weight, I found it impossible to try and treat it like a medium-sized fish. Instead I had to play it as though it were a real record-breaker.

I lost count of the number of runs it made, but gradually the rod began to take its strength away until I eventually had it on a short line directly astern of the boat. Even then it was not beaten completely. Three times I had the trace swivel hard up against the rod tip, and each time the gaffman had to let the trace loose again as the fish tore away from the boat. Finally, however, it was over. The fish was up and wallowing on the surface, its body a lovely violet colour in the sunlight, its neat jaw sagging open, the gill slits working slowly and the big tail flopping wearily with the action of the waves. This time the trace swivel came up to the rod tip and stayed there, while the skipper got hold of the trace for the fourth and last time. Slowly, inch by inch, the trace came over the side, and the gaff went hard in under the shark's gill slits. As I put down the rod and picked up the tail rope, someone whispered 'Half an hour'. Only thirty minutes fight.

I found the short length of time hard to believe, for in half an hour that gallant fish had made me work harder than practically any shark I had ever hooked in British waters. And what did it weigh? — 150, 200 lb? No, just 80 lb. It was quite tiny in comparison to many of the shark I have caught, but what a fighter. I doubt whether I will ever forget this fish and its unbelievable fighting spirit. Even in the boat, its gills mutilated by the flying gaff head, it continued to thrash about like a mad thing until I finally put it out of its misery with a well-aimed hammer blow on the end of its short neat snout. Maybe one day I will be fortunate enough to hook a really big thresher shark. If and when that great day comes, I hope I am using a reel with enough line on it to control the fish as it races away for freedom. If my 80-pounder was anything to go by, a really big thresher could be a truly formidable opponent.

Very little is really known about thresher shark, although I am convinced that they are far more common than is generally supposed. I am equally certain that thresher shark are hooked fairly frequently by bottom fishermen out after tope or skate with large fish baits. In my area alone, I regularly talk to anglers who have hooked fish on fairly substantial tackle only to discover that no matter how much pressure they apply, their fish just carries on going until either the rod or the line breaks. Threshers could also be responsible for smashing up beach anglers' tackle, as there have been many reports of big threshers feeding in water not much deeper than their body depth. Off Milford and Highcliffe beach in Hampshire, for example, anglers using whole fish baits for bass or tope quite frequently find themselves attached to something they cannot control at all.

I do not say that all these mystery fish are threshers, but some of them may well be. It is well known that these shark feed along this particular stretch of shoreline on occasion, and it is only reasonable to suppose that they will sometimes pick up an angler's bait. I know that large thresher patrol certain steep beaches along the south coast, Chesil Beach beyond Portland being a typical example.

Practically nothing constructive is known about thresher shark in general, and almost everything which has as yet been written about this species is either of purely local importance, or is in many cases pure supposition on the part of the writer. My own experiences with thresher shark along various stretches of the Hampshire coastline have led me to believe that they normally live and feed in moderate depths, preferably over flat sandy ground. Under these circumstances, I am fairly sure that these shark exist by preying on flatfish of one sort of another, or on round fish like pouting, whiting and pollack. When mackerel are shoaling thickly on or close to the surface, these shark often rise up to take full advantage of an easy meal. It is at these times – when on the hunt for mackerel – that they are sighted churning about on the surface.

Most rod-caught threshers fall to standard shark fishing baits and tackle, which to my mind make them accidental catches. I am convinced that under normal circumstances it would pay to fish for threshers with baits presented either directly on, or very close to the sea bed. No shark angler had as yet tried to catch thresher shark seriously and on a regular basis. This is probably because it is easier to go out with the intention of catching blue or porbeagle shark, when one knows full well that both these fish can usually be found without wasting too many totally blank days. Any angler who can afford the time to pursue thresher shark on a serious basis could no doubt succeed in catching these fish, by concentrating on an area where they have been frequently sighted by commercial boats.

I believe that once a likely locality has been selected, these shark could be caught by drifting with a small flatfish or round-fish on a long-running leger rig. Alternatively, it might well be possible to anchor the boat over a likely haunt, the bait again being fished hard on the bottom. One of the drawbacks to fishing at anchor, however, is the speed with which a big thresher continually changes direction, often circling the boat in the process. Other disadvantages, such as the possibility of a running fish fouling the anchor warp, are discussed in a later section of this book, 'Fishing from an Anchored Boat'. A further alternative is to drift in the conventional shark style, with the bait suspended just above the sea bed by a balloon or similar float.

I tried this technique seven or eight seasons ago in Freshwater Bay on the Isle of Wight. We had been out all night in search of big skate, and had in fact managed to boat an immense bottle-nose ray weighing exactly 110 lb. Fired by this success and by the fact that a number of threshers had been reported in the area only a day or two before our trip, we decided to go off out at dawn and try a drift in the area where the shark had been seen. The outside edge of Freshwater Bay is a great place for tope and I frankly expected to hook one of these rather than a shark. Even so, I set the bait at about eight to ten feet above the sea bed and we started to drift in a south-easterly direction. We were in the middle of a neap tide and the drift was very slow indeed. This suited us perfectly, for with the exertions of the night battle against the monstrous bottle-nosed ray and the warmth of the early morning sunshine we were all inclined to fall asleep and not to fish very seriously.

Half an hour elapsed with no sign of shark and, gradually lulled by the gentle slap of water and the warm sun, we all began to nod off. How long we dozed in this fashion I do not really know, but I was suddenly brought to my senses by a strange high-pitched buzzing sound. As I came to, I looked instinctively at my reel and saw to my amazement that the line was peeling off the spool at a considerable rate of knots. Leaping to my feet, I picked up the bucking rod and looked for my balloon float. The flat-calm surface of the water was absolutely deserted. Then suddenly, up popped my float, bobbed twice and went down again in a sideways lunge.

By this time I had the reel in gear, and as the line snapped taut I leaned back on the rod and set the hook. I immediately wished that I had not, for the fish went off in a long and quite unbelievably fast run. I only had a medium-weight rod and 45 lb BS line, and as the fish ran on I soon realized just how puny my tackle was in comparison to the monster I had hooked. Looking back now, I realize that I must have still been half-asleep, otherwise I would never have tried to slow the fish down by tightening up the star-drag mechanism on my big multi-plying reel. I still had plenty of line in hand, but I did not think of this as I tried to manhandle a fish that was far too powerful to control during its first mad rush for freedom.

I realized my mistake the moment the running line pulled up tight, but before I could even attempt to slacken off my reel drag I felt the line part and then fall slack as the fish got away. Two hundred yards away, my balloon suddenly surfaced, and beyond that I caught a brief glimpse of a flurry of white water as a big fish momentarily broke surface. I have always been convinced that this particular shark was a thresher. Its terrible turn of speed alone proved to me it was not a porbeagle. It is true that it did not at any time jump, but a fish hooked close to the bottom in eighty feet of water would be unlikely to jump anyway. Given time it would have maybe cleared the surface, but since the whole episode only took a minute or two I doubt whether the fish even had time to think of leaping out of the water in an attempt to shake the hook free from his jaw.

This was my first and last serious attempt to go out with thresher in mind, as porbeagles have taken up most of my time since this particular encounter. However, I think I proved a point, even though I lost the fish within minutes of striking it. Maybe sometime in the near future I will be able to devote a whole season's sharking to trying to catch threshers in quantity, from localities which these grand fish are known to inhabit. If I do, then I may be lucky enough to prove some definite points about this particular breed. Only time and consistent fishing in the right areas can help to solve the general mystery which surrounds them, as at present we are all in the dark about their overall movement and general feeding habits.

The present thresher shark record has stood at 180 lb since 1933. The captor of this fish, who once held the British rod-caught conger record, boated his thresher off Dungeness on the Kent coast. Practically no details are known about its capture, except that it was hooked on a bait fished right on the bottom. I am fairly sure that once again this was an 'accidental' fish, taken on a bait intended for some other species. The mere fact that this record has already stood for almost forty years shows just how few threshers are ever caught and how very little we know about them. With the exception of a few other thresher shark over 200 lb, the only other specimens caught have all been on the small side.

Oddly enough, threshers definitely show interest in artificial baits, and feathers in particular seem to attract them. I doubt whether a season goes by on the Isle of Wight grounds without at least half a dozen threshers being hooked by anglers feather-ing for mackerel, and in all cases at least one of the feather hooks is actually right in the shark's mouth. This proves fairly con-clusively that the fish try to snap at the feathers, rather than swimming into them by accident and becoming foul-hooked as the anglers pull up the rod. Many people believe that these sharks snatch at mackerel already caught on the feather lines. This is quite possible, but all the anglers I have spoken to, who have hit threshers on mackerel feathers, have assured me that when the shark struck there were no mackerel on the lines at all. It may well be possible to catch these shark on specially con-structed feather flights, but I doubt very much whether any angler could be persuaded to go out deliberately feathering for sharks. Large weighted feather lures might well work if trolled deep down and slowly behind a moving boat, and this aspect of sharking is discussed in the section, 'Trolling'.

Having tasted at first hand the thrills of playing a good sized thresher, I am convinced in my own mind that no other shark, not even the mighty mako, can match the firework display put up by an angry thresher. Each time I go out after shark I hope that I have the good fortune to set a hook into one of the really large threshers which lurk off my local stretch of coastline. No doubt the day will come when I do hit one of these monsters, and when it does I hope I am able to beat the shark into submission. Threshers are worthy opponents for any shark angler and as such they are well worth hunting down.

Shark Attacks

Several of our common sharks are suspected of being man-eaters in tropical waters, but until 1971 no definite attacks had ever been recorded off the coasts of Great Britain. Then, in the space of four weeks, two attacks were recorded, both from shallow water and both potentially very dangerous.

The first attack was on a skin diver who was quietly working his way out from the beach at Beesand, South Devon. In this case, the shark responsible was thought to be a porbeagle. Fortunately, the diver was able to fend off two attacks without suffering anything worse than shock, and before the shark came back for the third time, he managed to swim into water too shallow for it to follow. The second attack took place on the Kent coast. On this occasion, a pair of large threshers attacked a child who was swimming in very shallow water. Once again the sharks failed to inflict any serious damage on their victim, although the child was knocked about rather badly by their tails and bodies.

I am inclined to think that this second attack was more of an accidental meeting than a deliberate attempt at man-eating. On the other hand, eye-witnesses to the first attack were absolutely certain that the shark quite definitely and deliberately tried to savage the unfortunate skin diver. The same witnesses and the diver estimated the shark's length at around twelve feet. A porbeagle of this size would weigh about 1,000 lb, or at least 670 lb more than the existing rod-caught record. Quite apart from these two widespread incidents, several other shark scares

Ted Belston with one of the mako sharks he caught from the Falmouth boat *Huntress*, skippered by R. Vinnicombe

A big blue shark weighing well over 100 lb turns away from the boat

The jaws of a blue shark caught by the author off Looe

An Isle of Wight porbeagle – well beaten and ready for the gaff

The flying gaff neatly hooked in between the fins of 200 lb
of angry porbeagle

One of the first blue sharks caught by the author – fresh from
the sea off Mevagissey

were recorded during June and July of 1971, the most note-worthy being at Southsea, where bathers were advised to leave the water due to several biggish sharks which spent a whole day patrolling up and down a popular bathing beach.

I doubt whether sharks will ever be regarded as a serious menace in our seas, but at the same time it does not do to underestimate these creatures – which are unpredictable at the best of times. Many times when sharks have come sniffing up to my boat at sea, I have thought that anyone foolish enough to fall into the water could find themselves in serious trouble, particularly when the fish go on a mad feeding spree, stimulated by a particularly smelly trail of rubby-dubby. It is not until you find yourself in a boat surrounded by a pack of biggish porbeagles, which continually try to tear the rubby-dubby bag off its rope, that you begin to realize that sharks in the throes of a real feeding frenzy show no fear of anything alive or dead. This is when they are at their most dangerous and when they could easily turn into man-killers, should anyone be unlucky enough to fall amongst them.

The Gear for the Job ...

Lines and Reels
Rods
Rings and Reel-fittings
Hooks and Traces
Gaffs and Tailers
Shark Boats
Rubby-Dubby
Bait

Lines and Reels

During the past two or three seasons, the wind of change has blown steadily over the sport of shark fishing. New grounds have been discovered and developed and new sharking techniques have been devised to overcome the problems presented by these new-found sharking hot-spots. Naturally enough, new ideas on shark tackle have been aired with the result that traditional sharking rods, reels and lines have come in for a fair amount of practical criticism. I am glad to say that this has led to the production of some first-class tackle which, although still open to further change, has in fact gone a long way to improve the standard of tackle generally used by British shark fishermen.

Traditionally, the shark is a brute of a fish which can only be taken on really heavy-weight tackle. This sort of outdated belief has been fostered for many years by shark-boat skippers who supply hire tackle as part of their service to customers.

Unfortunately, novice anglers trying shark-fishing for the first time have hired this tackle, caught a shark or two and then, in the mistaken belief that they are buying the correct gear, have gone out and purchased an identical outfit to the one supplied by their boatman. When it is too late, they discover that in fact they have bought an outfit which is far too heavy and cumbersome to use in comfort, but by this time their financial outlay has been so great that they make do and soldier on rather than cutting their losses and choosing a more suitable set.

One cannot blame the boatmen for this state of affairs since their object is to boat any fish which is hooked by their clients; and since most of the anglers they take out know very little about playing a big fish, they naturally equip their boats with the strongest rods, reels and lines they can obtain. Obviously a charter-boat skipper's reputation is only as good as the fish he brings in, and although many would prefer their anglers to fish light, they just cannot afford to take the chance of losing a big shark through a novice smashing a rod and line.

Although by no means a new sport, big-game fishing for shark in British waters is still in its infancy, and English anglers on the whole lag far behind their American counterparts as far as tackle is concerned. The Americans have already taken to extremes the art of light-tackle fishing for shark, tuna and billfish, but in England we are now only just beginning to realize that it is possible to catch big shark on truly sporting tackle. The introduction of International Game Fishing Association approved lines has gone a long way to further sport fishing for shark in British waters, and as IGFA class lines are now readily available to any British angler, most truly knowledgeable shark fishermen are adopting them for general use.

IGFA class lines are tested to break at or just before their stated BS; a 50 lb class line, for example, should part on a 48–49 lb pull. This means that when an angler uses an IGFA class line to catch a big fish, the line itself has no extra tolerance above the stated breaking strain. Other lines, such as Sea

Ranger, which are not manufactured to correspond with IGFA rulings, often have an actual BS of twenty per cent or even more above their stated BS. I have carried out extensive tests on several popular lines that do not carry IGFA ratings and in many cases have found that a line alleged to break on a direct 80 lb pull will in fact withstand a pull well in excess of 100 lb. These sort of lines obviously give even the most hamfisted anglers every chance of horsing a big fish up to the gaff without fear of a break, whereas the class lines call for a great deal of skill.

The idea of using IGFA class lines for shark fishing in British waters is without doubt a most exciting one, for it sets a standard which many experienced shark anglers will wish to follow. More important still, it will give newcomers to the sport the idea that they can fish for and successfully catch very big shark on ultra-light lines. In many cases this will mean that British shark fishermen will now be able to compete with American anglers for the privilege of breaking both open and existing world records for given line strengths. Vince Lister of Poole has already begun to experiment with IGFA class lines, and in his first season on the Isle of Wight grounds he boated several potential world records on 12 lb class lines.

The idea of catching big shark on lines that break on a pull of only 12–15 lb may well seem strange to anglers used to fishing 80–100 lb lines, but in time I am quite certain that shark fishermen all round the country will come to accept the general use of light line as normal procedure. When this finally occurs, shark angling will become a real game fishing sport. In Australian waters, shark of well over 1,000 lb weight have already been taken on lines with a BS of only 20 lb. If fish of this calibre can be subdued on tackle as light as this, I can see no valid reason why 100 lb fish cannot be taken on 12–20 lb line by British anglers. The only disadvantage to the ultra-light tackle is that, no matter how good an angler one may be, a high percentage of hooked fish will manage to break free at some stage of the battle, which means that the lost fish make off trailing a wire trace and yards of line.

At the moment no one is sure whether or not these 'lost' fish die or recover. One thing is certain, however: shark are rarely caught containing hooks or traces. Thus, lost fish must either manage to get rid of this tackle, or else die as a direct result of swallowing it. When one sees some of the terrible scars that shark carry on their bodies, it is hard to believe that the presence of a hook and a length of wire in their mouth or throat can cause them any damage. On the other hand, shark experts from both sides of the Atlantic argue that, despite their hard tough bodies and obvious physical strength, shark of all types are nervous fish which die easily from shock and nervous exhaustion. Only time can tell whether this is so. I am personally inclined to believe that the bulk of such fish do manage to live through the experience, and shed the trailing hook and trace without undue difficulty.

One thing is sure: the light-tackle man must be prepared to lose a high proportion of hooked fish before he successfully boats his first possible record-beater. I well remember my initial experiences of light-tackle fishing for porbeagles off the Isle of Wight. The day was good with an unusually gentle breeze which just ruffled the otherwise smooth water. Our boat was drifting slowly to the south-west of the overfall area, and we had three sets of tackle out to take good advantage of the wide, oily rubby-dubby trail, washing steadily out of the mesh bag tied midway down the boat. As usual the shark arrived suddenly and in a pack, and the first fish hit hard at the double-mackerel bait mounted on standard-weight shark tackle. Unfortunately, this first run came to nothing, as the fish ejected the bait after making a fast but unhittable run.

The other two baits had been drawn in the moment the run occurred, and as I picked up my bait and looked over the gunwale the water seemed to be alive with shark. At least four individual fish could be seen, twisting and turning just below the rubby-dubby bag. As I lowered my bait into the water, one big dorsal fin broke surface and made straight at the bait as it began to sink through the oil slick. Under normal circumstances I would have been delighted, but with only 20 lb BS line on the reel, I suddenly realized how little chance I stood against this fish. Through the clear water I saw it hit the bait and turn down at speed, and I knew for certain that this fish would smash me on the first run. I expected a break to occur, but not quite as quickly as it did. As the fish went down, the few feet of slack line and trace came tight at terrific speed and before the reel even gave a half-turn the line parted at the rod tip with an audible crack.

Ten minutes later, with shark still swarming round the boat, I was ready for a second go with a new trace and bright shiny bait. Once again the bait was taken within seconds of hitting the water, but this time I had the star drag right off. With the reel practically free-spooling, I watched yard after yard of line melt off the reel. Initially, with over 800 yards of line to play with, I felt fairly confident of my ability to check this first run. However, as the fish continued to plough steadily on, and as my original stock of line became rapidly depleted, I began to worry that the fish would simply run out every inch of line on the reel until it came to the knot. A brief attempt at thumbing the spool, to try to apply enough pressure to turn the fish, proved conclusively that this tactic was a waste of time. The added pressure of my thumb seemed to spur the fish on to greater efforts and to a turn of speed which swallowed line at a tremendous rate. With over 400 yards of line out, the exposed silver sides of my reel spool were a grim reminder that unless the fish turned soon I would lose it.

By this stage the boat's engine was running, and at a signal from me the skipper opened up the throttle to try to run up on the fish, so that I could recover as much line as possible. As an absolute novice in this light-line game fishing, I was learning new tricks with every yard of line I gained or lost. It became obvious that we should have chased the fish from the moment I struck the hook home. Fortunately, this particular shark stayed close to the surface, instead of diving deep down as many porbeagles do, and I am sure this is what enabled me to hold it for the crucial stages of the fight. A 20 lb line and very light boat rod does not let the angler apply a great deal of pressure, and so apart from one or two early attempts to give this particular fish as much stick as possible, I quickly settled down to the idea that I was in for a long, slow battle, with most of the luck on the shark's side.

It hit surface twice during the early stages of the struggle, but although a big fish thrashing about on the surface can easily roll up in the trace and break the reel line, I was content to let this one stay on top. Once it got its head down, the strength of the fish plus the increased water pressure would have been far too much for the light line to stand. Time goes by very quickly when one is playing a large fish, and having prepared myself for a long fight, I was quite happy to let the shark keep an even 100 yards in front of the boat. I knew that the drag of the line and the constant light rod pressure would finally wear it down so that we could take the chance of gaffing it. Although this was my first light-line shark, I quickly became accustomed to the technique of playing it. A combination of careful boat handling and gentle but firm handling of the tackle made it weaken visibly, less than one-and-a-half hours after it had first been struck.

I could sense the growing tiredness of the fish long before I could manage to gain line on it. This transmission of increasing weakness led me to build up rod pressure gradually, until I knew for certain that the shark was losing ground. There is a terrific feeling of achievement when one gains line on a well-beaten fish, and as the reel spool began to retrieve line, inch by inch, I felt for the first time that, light line or not, this fish was going to be mine. Inches turned into feet, and then yards, and as the distance between boat and fish began rapidly to decrease, my companions started to make preparations for the gaffing. With less than twenty yards of line to recover, the shark surfaced once more, for the last time.

As it swam into clear view, I could not help but feel a pang of regret at its obvious exhaustion. Not a big fish, it still fought on against rod pressure, its big tail lashing feebly back and forth as it tried to generate enough energy to escape from the pursuing boat. Finally, more dead than alive, it floated alongside and the first gaff sank home. There was no need for a tail rope on this one. Its lack of size and total exhaustion rendered it incapable of any last minute fireworks. It was so tired that in fact it barely moved as it came over the gunwales, and in many ways I was sorry that this grand little fish had fought so hard and long to die so quietly on the gaff. That shark weighed in at just on 70 lb. Minute in comparison to some of the monsters that lurk off the Isle of Wight, it was nevertheless my first light-tackle 'beagle', and a fish that I shall never regret.

Obviously, light-tackle shark fishing with an eye to possible world records is not every angler's idea of sport, but it has a great deal of potential, particularly for the more experienced shark man. Having caught my first fish on light gear, I tried the technique on other occasions as well. Experience showed that, maybe through lack of light-tackle experience, I in fact lost many of the shark I hooked, usually during the first sixty seconds of the fight. The fish I did bring to the gaff were all well under the 100 lb mark and I came to the conclusion that anything much over this weight was almost impossible to handle, unless it made the mistake of staying close to the surface throughout the entire battle.

I saw several fish break the reel line as they took the bait, and it seemed to me that even small multipliers like the Penn Longbeach or Garcia 624 had drags too fierce for the line strengths. Short of holding the rod at all times and knocking the reel into the free-spool position the moment a shark hits the bait, I can see no way as yet of overcoming this problem. Time and experience of light-line shark fishing will no doubt iron out many of the present drawbacks to this style of angling, and I have no doubt that it will in due course of time become a well-established sport with British anglers.

As far as general shark fishing is concerned, it is difficult to lay down hard and fast rules as to what is exactly needed. Final choice of tackle depends on a great many things, the most important being the type of shark you are most likely to catch, and the area you intend to fish. If, for example, blues are your main quarry and you fish a section of coast where the average fish weighs 50–70 lb, a medium-weight boat rod and 6-0 size reel, loaded with 60 lb BS line, should successfully boat practically every fish you hook. Many anglers assume quite incorrectly that it is impossible to catch even medium-sized blue shark on tackle of this calibre. However, since most tope anglers fish with much smaller reels and lines of half the BS, for fish which can easily top the 60 lb mark, it seems quite ridiculous to fish for shark of similar size with heavy-weight tackle.

One of the drawbacks to using light tackle on the blue shark grounds is that there is always the chance possibility of a big mako, porbeagle or even a thresher taking the bait and subsequently breaking the line. Personally, I find that this sort of thing occurs so infrequently that when it does happen I simply accept the loss of the fish as part of the game. I would rather catch the bulk of my blue shark on tackle which will allow them to show some fighting spirit, than to skuldrag most of them to the gaff on tackle designed only for the very occasional big shark.

Choice of tackle for use on porbeagle and thresher grounds is slightly more complex. Practically every experienced big shark catcher has his own likes and dislikes, and wherever a group of knowledgeable shark men meet, the difference of opinions on tackle is colossal. At present, American reels are very much in favour. Penn Senators in the 9-0 to 12-0 range are the most popular, although Everol and the Japanese-made Roddy Dominator are much favoured by those anglers fortunate enough to be able to afford them. Garcia have also devised a special game-fishing reel, but at a cost of over £100 it is beyond the average angler's pocket.

For my own big shark fishing, I find the Grice and Young Tatler V ideal, although I also carry and occasionally use a Senator 9–0. The Tatler is a medium-priced reel with many features which make it first-class for sharking. Its only disadvantage is that it only comes in the 6–0 size, which limits its line capacity in comparison to that of a 9–0 reel. Even so, the wide compression-moulded, fibre-glass spool of the Tatler holds over 400 yards of 60 lb BS dacron, or just on 300 yards of 80 lb BS. Many shark anglers regard the Tatler as rather a small reel for big shark. It has, however, accounted for mako of up to 476 lb in Cornish waters, and South African fishermen buy it in preference to most other game fishing reels. Lightness is one of its chief advantages, and when it comes to a long and arduous battle with a big strong fish, the overall weight of rod and reel can make a big difference to the angler. Tackle balance can also matter a great deal, and I find that the wide low build of the Tatler makes for truly comfortable fishing. This is an aspect which many anglers overlook when choosing a reel, but it is a point well worth taking into consideration. I now use Tatler reels for the bulk of my big shark fishing, and after several hard seasons sharking can find nothing to complain about in their construction.

Several centre pin reels are produced for the shark fishing market, the Noris Shakespeare Leviathan being the most widely used. This is serviceable enough but is extremely heavy, which makes for tiring fishing. The Leviathan incorporates a drag mechanism similar to that of a multiplying reel. This has the advantage of allowing the reel drum to revolve while the handle remains stationary. Other large centre pins do not incorporate this refinement, and consequently when a big fish takes off on a long run the big handles revolve at the same speed as the spool. When this happens, woe betide the angler who does not get his fingers out of the way in time, for the heavy handle can easily skin or break any fingers it contacts. The Leviathan is also fitted with a lever brake system which allows the angler to apply extra pressure to a running fish.

Hardy Brothers once produced a superb centre pin reel for big game fishing. Known as 'The Fortuna', this reel was a masterpiece of engineering skill. Unfortunately, they are no longer manufactured, although occasional models in good condition sometimes occur in sporting sales, or in fishing tackle shops which specialize in second-hand equipment. Nowadays, these reels are usually snapped up as soon as they come on the market, and often at a very fancy price. Even so, any angler who manages to find one in good condition would be well advised to buy it, for as a general shark or big game reel the Fortuna cannot, in my opinion, be equalled. Line capacity is one of the major advantages of a big centre pin reel, and a standard Fortuna should hold 600–800 yards of 80 lb line with ease. This huge capacity plus its unique star drag system make it an absolute pleasure to use for all forms of sharking.

Shark fishermen are usually extremely fussy about lines, and in most cases they favour a braided line constructed from either Terylene or Polyester fibre. Both materials are expensive, and to load a reel with, say, 400 yards of 60 lb or 80 lb braided line will cost well over £6. Nylon lines are not popular since heavy nylon has a tendency to sink, and unless great care is taken it quickly drops down to become entangled with the trace and bait. This may not be apparent to the angler until a shark picks up the bait plus the unprotected nylon, and cuts the line on its first short run. Being more buoyant and less inclined to stretch, braided lines do not suffer from this particular fault, and consequently are very popular with the experienced angler.

Braided Terylene is now less popular than the American-made Polyester fibre lines. Polyester is in fact more supple than the rather coarse Terylene, and is thinner strain for strain in overall diameter. This is an important point in its favour as it allows the angler space on the reel for an extra hundred yards or so of line. I use Dacron line of this type on my Penn Senator 9-0 reel, and find I can use exactly 600 yards to fill the reel spool comfortably. Before switching to this line I used Terylene of similar BS and found 400 yards was as much as the reel could hold. Braided lines have the added advantage of being practically rot-proof, and thus although the initial outlay may seem exorbitant, it should last over several seasons, spreading the cost. Its main disadvantage is that it knots badly, and unless a special knot known as a 'hangman's jam' is used, the line will often cut itself when subjected to strain.

Rods

Practically every tackle company in the country produces a rod which they claim is suitable for shark fishing. Being a tackle dealer, I naturally see many of these rods and, to be honest, a good many are little more than flashy rubbish. Shark rods vary considerably in price, but one can pay anything from £9 to £30 for a good rod, with an average rod costing between £16 and £20. Rod prices vary, of course, according to the quality of the rod blank and the various fittings, but the best is usually the cheapest in the long run.

Test curves as such will not be of much interest to the average shark fisherman, although some rod builders now take the trouble to put the test curve figure on the rods they manufacture. Most shark rods have a rating of 30-60 lb. Three times the stated figure gives a rough rating of the strength of line that can be used with the rod in question. Thus, in the case of a rod with a 25 lb test curve, lines of up to 75 lb can be used. Actually, one can allow thirty per cent either way of this figure, and in fact lines with a BS of 30-75 lb can be employed.

Until quite recently, the majority of British-made shark rods measured approximately six feet. Progressive rod manufacturers, however, are now building rods of seven feet or more in overall length, and no doubt in time even longer rods will become available. Personally I am in favour of these longer rods, for shark, and particularly porbeagles, have a nasty habit of trying to take cover underneath the boat. When this happens, short rods seldom have enough leverage to work the fish away. The long rods, on the other hand, can usually be relied upon to turn the fish before it can get under the boat.

In the early days of the Isle of Wight sharking, I lost a very good fish indeed while using a standard six-foot shark rod. This particular fish had been played for close to three-quarters of an hour, during which time it had been well and truly thrashed. Finally, just as my companion was preparing to use the big gaff, the shark managed to summon up enough strength to wriggle down under the boat, where it stopped to sulk. Needless to say, I tried every trick in the book in an attempt to shift it out into the open, but the short rod just did not have the length required to drag it out. Eventually, the wire trace caught on the propeller and the fish broke free. This experience taught me that a short rod has definite limitations and at the first opportunity I changed to a longer rod, which in subsequent seasons has served me very well indeed.

When choosing a shark rod, one should bear in mind that it will be subjected to far more stresses and strains than an ordinary boat rod. Consequently, it pays to make sure that it has been built by a firm which has a reputation for quality. Shark rods are nowadays constructed of glass blanks, either of a solid or tubular construction. The better-class rods are invariably made up from tubular blanks, combining strength with overall lightness which is an essential combination where big fish are concerned. Carbon fibre rods are also being developed, but as no one has as yet produced a carbon fibre shark rod this new material is still an unknown quantity. The new Hardy Saltwater Range incorporates an interesting feature, which appears to give a light rod a terrific amount of lifting power in the butt section. This is achieved by double-wrapping the fibreglass on the butt section of the blank, building up the actual wall thickness of the glass to such an extent that it can lift a great deal of weight without undue strain on the rod.

Rings and Reel-fittings

All anglers are inclined to buy a rod for its overall appearance, and consequently those with flashy rings and shiny chromed fittings are very popular. Unfortunately, all that glitters is not gold and the corrosive effects of salt water soon turn a glossy beautiful rod into a rusty tarnished wreck. Because of this problem, the angler who is on the lookout for a new, heavy shark or boat rod will be well advised to pay careful attention to the metalwork, and under no circumstances should he be blinded by its overall appearance as it hangs in the tackle shop. In my early days I fell into this trap and purchased several rods which I had to refurnish completely at the end of their first season's use.

Shark anglers give a rod a heavy caning at the best of times, and as yet few manufacturers are building models to withstand the rigours of this hard fishing. Hardy Bros, Constable, and Davenport and Fordham are the main builders of really top-quality equipment, and for the main part they all fit their rods with identical rings and reel fittings. Stainless-steel reel fittings are the best, as they do not corrode when exposed to salt water and, when compared to chromed brass, seem less inclined to seize up.

Quality rods nearly always incorporate roller rings in their make-up, the best being the Aftco brand which, although very expensive, cannot be faulted in any way. Shark anglers can never agree as to whether a rod should possess a full set of roller guides, or simply a butt and tip roller with hardened steel, or lined intermediate rings. I favour the latter, for a full set of rollers adds considerably to the cost of a rod and in my opinion serves no really useful purpose.

At the end of a day's fishing it pays to wash a rod and all its fittings in fresh water, paying strict attention to the more inaccessible corners where salt can collect. Once thoroughly rinsed off, the rod can be wiped dry with a soft cloth, and then rubbed over with another cloth and a drop of light machine oil. This will help protect all the fittings and should add years to its life.

Hooks and Traces

Even a medium-sized shark has a large, strong-jawed mouth, armed with innumerable sharp, neat teeth which are more than capable of cutting right through anything other than a heavy wire trace. A big shark has even more formidable jaws, and as most anglers go sharking with the definite intention of catching the largest specimens they can locate, it is essential that their traces and hooks should be made from the best and most robust materials available. Trace wire is of prime importance, yet far too many anglers concentrate on obtaining the finest rods, reels and lines available, and penny-pinch over their terminal tackle. This is a common fault and a silly one, for no matter how strong or how expensive a rod, reel or line may be, it is the trace and hook which take all the severe punishment during a prolonged fight with a big shark. Unless these are up to scratch, all the quality rods and reels in the world will not save you from losing the bulk of the fish you hook.

At present, nylon-covered wire is widely used for traces. This can be obtained in strains of up to 250 lb and many anglers use it with confidence until they lose fish, when they realize that it is not all that the manufacturers claim it to be. For one thing, nylon-covered wire is expensive to buy and very prone to kinking. Worse still, it chafes badly when rubbed against the rough hide of a shark, and should in fact be discarded as soon as the nylon sheath begins to wear. This means that in most cases a trace can only be used to catch one fish before it becomes unsafe to use. Again, the nylon sheath is soft enough to catch on a shark's teeth, which gives the fish a ninety per cent chance of cutting through the inner wire long before it can be brought to the gaff.

Several years ago, I carried out extensive tests with this kind of wire for blue and porbeagle shark, both in this country and off Southern Ireland. During these tests I lost far more shark than I boated and on each occasion I found the trace bitten through close to the hook and the nylon covering pushed back to expose the bare wire. Evidently, when the fish had taken the bait, the hook had engaged well back inside the mouth, leaving the trace protruding over the sharp teeth. As the fish swam away from the boat, with the remainder of the trace stretched out behind it, the wire in its mouth hooked round one or more of the teeth, forming an acute angle. The teeth cut into the nylon sheath which then jammed, allowing the shark to gnaw away at one tiny section of the unprotected wire.

Having established this weakness to my own satisfaction, I switched to a trace material made of twisted-wire cabling of the type used for light boat rigging. Since making this change, I have had no loss of fish due to wire parting either against the fish's teeth or through rod pressure. More important still, the cable trace can be used over and over again. As I have said, nylon-covered wire can seldom be used more than once, and as it is expensive to buy in the first place it can become a costly business when one discards each trace after each session.

The local yacht chandlery at Lymington makes up all my traces at a fraction of the cost a normal tackle shop would charge and, even more important, works to my own specifications, using the hooks and swivels which I favour most. Length of trace is a very important factor to consider. Shark of all kinds have a habit of rolling themselves up in a trace, and if too short a length of wire is used the rough body of the fish quickly comes into direct contact with the reel line directly above it, leading almost inevitably to a break. Twelve feet is the absolute minimum length and I have mine made up in fourteen- and sixteen-foot lengths. Some anglers use longer traces, but I find that, even with the extra long shark rods I use, any trace over sixteen feet long becomes practically unmanageable when the fish is alongside the boat ready for gaffing.

A good shark trace should be furnished with at least two large, durable barrel swivels. Some anglers use three, but I prefer to stick to two, breaking the trace into equal lengths joined exactly in the middle by a swivel. Swivels are essential to counteract the twists and turns a shark makes as it is being played out. I do not worry too much about testing these to ascertain their exact BS when under tension, for I feel that almost any 5–0 size brass-barrel swivel will support a dead weight of well over 100 lb. As I use lines well below this BS, anything that snaps while a fish is being played is almost certain to be the reel line. Thus, I can see no valid reason for paying out on expensive swivels, tested to break from 200–300 lb, when a cheaper model will do the job just as well.

Hooks are of course very important and it is unfortunate that we do not have many patterns to choose between in this country. The Mustad Seamaster is the only truly suitable shark hook on sale in Great Britain. Fortunately, it is a good hook, ideal in many ways for the kind of shark fishing we do. I favour the 12–0 size for all my shark fishing, but in West-Country waters many anglers use 10–0 hooks when going after blues. The Seamaster hook is available in sizes up to 16–0, but I feel these giant hooks have no real use for general sharking except on rare occasions when exceptionally large baits are being used.

Newcomers to shark fishing often purchase extra-large hooks in the belief that they are ideal for all forms of sharking. This is totally wrong, and leads to a lot of lost fish and dropped baits. Shark are no fools, and if they pick up a bait mounted on a huge hook they quickly become suspicious of its unnatural hardness, and drop the fish long before the angler has a chance to set the hook. 12–0 hooks, being comparatively small, fit neatly into a bait and have the great advantage of being easy to set on the strike, especially when well sharpened with a coarse carborundum stone. 14–0 and 16–0 hooks are difficult to drive into a fish with a normal shark rod, even when honed to a razor's-edge degree of sharpness, and I have known more fish lost from these hooks than from the smaller size.

Many anglers make the mistake of only striking once at a biting fish. This habit can often lead to lost shark, and to make absolutely certain that the hook is well set it pays to strike hard three or four times in quick succession, reeling in the resulting slack line between every strike, so that the shark is on a tight line each time the rod sweeps back.

Gaffs and Tailers

West-Country shark boats are normally equipped with fixed gaffs, or in fact those which have the actual gaff head pinned firmly to the wooden handle. This sort of gaff is perfectly adequate when dealing with small and medium-sized blues, but is far from ideal when used against big shark, as many an angler and skipper has found out to his personal cost. In the early days of sharking off the Isle of Wight, fixed gaffs were found to be extremely dangerous, and nowadays most Island shark boats carry break-away gaffs.

Grice and Young of Christchurch, Hampshire, make the only good break-away or flying gaff that I have ever come across. This superb instrument is made up of 80 tons B S tensile stainless steel, fitted to a six-foot, shaped handle. The gaff head itself is attached to ten feet of rope and steel cable, making the whole gaff a lethal yet extremely simple instrument to use. The manufacturers of this gaff recommend that the breakaway head should be linked to the handle by a length of light line, which should snap the moment the gaff is driven well into the fish. This works well enough although I personally prefer to dispense with the light line entirely, holding the gaff in its socket by hauling on the rope and wire attached to the head. By keeping this tight, the head can be held firmly in place until the gaff is set; then, by relaxing pressure on the rope, the head will drop clear of the handle which can be brought inboard, leaving the shark thrashing at the end of a ten-foot rope and wire leader.

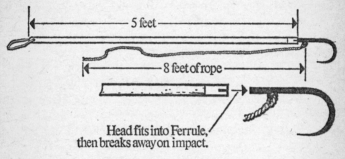

5 feet

8 feet of rope

Head fits into Ferrule, then breaks away on impact.

Break-away or flying gaff

Big shark tend to go raving mad the moment they feel the gaff head driven into their body. This gigantic flurry is the main reason why a flying gaff should be used, as when a shark begins to thrash no man will be able to hang on to a fixed handle for long, and five or six feet of heavy wood handle flailing about can break an arm or skull with one clout. With the fish on a length of pliable rope and wire, this danger is completely eliminated – although accidents do occasionally occur when someone foolishly winds the rope, or worse still the wire, around his hand.

A young Kent angler found out just how dangerous this can

be when, at the beginning of the 1971 shark season, he encountered a very big shark off Dover. At some stage of the
battle a wire rope was slipped over the fish and the excited
angler wrapped the wire right round his hand, trying to get
enough grip to drag it into the boat. At this stage, the shark
took on a new lease of life and took off at full speed in the
general direction of the French coast. The sudden pull of the
fish naturally snapped the wire right round the angler's fingers,
and for the next three-quarters of an hour the fish steamed on,
towing the boat and its two occupants behind it.

The young angler's hand was taking the entire strain of
both fish and boat, and for the full forty-five minutes he could
only stand helplessly by as the wire cut deeper and deeper into
his flesh. Fortunately, the fish then managed to get clear of the
wire, and its unfortunate victim – now more than a little in-
jured and naturally terribly frightened – was able to extricate
the wire from his hand while the other occupant of the boat
started the motor and headed back to port. No really serious
damage was done, although considerable hospital treatment
was required before the angler was allowed to go home. I doubt
very much whether this particular young man will ever make
the mistake of winding wire line or rope round his hand again,
and I hope that the resulting story will be a lesson to all
others.

The power of even a tired shark can be amazing. I remember
once watching a big shark gaffed far too soon by a skipper
operating off the Isle of Wight. The fish, which weighed in at
220 lb, had only been played for a few minutes when in typical
porbeagle fashion it swam lazily up to the boat. Seeing what
appeared to be an ideal opportunity to gaff the fish before it
really began to fight, the skipper drove the flying gaff home,
snatched out the handle and began heaving the rope. For the
first second or two the fish came easily. Then, whether in pain
or from fear, it suddenly went berserk. At the same instant the
taut wire snagged into a join in the gunwale. The fish ripped

away the whole of the top section before steaming off, the wire and rope trailing along its broad side with the angler still attached, trying to slow it down with rod pressure.

All this happened in split seconds, and although I saw the skipper make his lunge with the gaff, followed by the gunwale peeling off, it was not until I returned to port that I heard the full story. Apparently, after the initial gaffing during the first few minutes of the fight, the shark went on fighting for another three-quarters of an hour, despite the fact that it had a huge gaff head embedded in its belly. Finally, more dead than alive, it was dragged alongside for the second time, and the trailing gaff rope was secured and made fast to a stern post. The tail rope was then slipped into position and the fish was dragged over the wrecked gunwale into the boat. Even then, it went into a final frenzy, smashing several Thermos flasks and a box before it finally expired.

The tail rope is another essential piece of equipment for all shark boats, and in my opinion it is this that finishes all big shark battles easily and smoothly. I carry a special tailer made up from a length of medium-sized rigging wire attached to a seven-foot length of rope. The wire is made up in the form of a loop, so that it can be opened easily to slip over a big tail and snap tight again the moment it is in place. Rigging-wire tailers are much more manageable and effective than plain rope. Their stiffness and weight alone make them easy to slip over a wildly lashing tail, whereas a pliable and buoyant rope is difficult to manoeuvre and often impossible to keep open. Any wirework specialist will make up a wire tailer suitable for shark fishing, at a price which makes it about the best investment that any angler or skipper can make.

When it has been tailed correctly, a shark cannot possibly escape unless the angler or skipper does something really stupid, like tying the end of the tailer to a stern-post or cleat with a knot that slips or unravels under strain. Oddly enough, it is easy to make a mistake like this out of sheer excitement, and more than one big shark has gained its freedom in this way. A shark's big tail is its main means of motivation and once it is deprived of this source of power it become pretty helpless. As soon as its tail has been wired and lifted clear of the water the fish is just about finished, but until this stage is reached a gaffed and tailed shark can still put up one hell of a fight – even when held hard up against the side of a boat.

Shark Boats

In my opinion there is no such thing as an ideal shark-fishing boat as yet in use in this country. The Cornish are probably nearest to the best design with their traditional 'Tosher' style boat, with its forward-mounted engines and wheelhouse, its open cockpit, and its lug sail to hold it steady while drifting. Unfortunately, these boats are slow and although perfectly suitable for use in areas where the shark grounds are within an hour and a half's run from the shore, they are impractical for use off the Isle of Wight, for example, where an 8–10 knot boat might well take four hours to reach the grounds. Here something in the 15–20 knot class is essential. However, a big boat of say, 30 feet or more, capable of achieving these sort of speeds, is a very expensive craft to build. Moreover, although it is possible to obtain a variety of suitable hulls for getting out to the sharking areas quickly and efficiently, none of the high-speed hulls seems to be much good on the drift. Obviously, they are designed for speed and not for wallowing about on the surface, and this defect shows up the moment the engines are stopped. These craft bang and bob about all over the place, making the customers sick, and, worse still, seldom drifting on an even course, so that the rubby-dubby trail is continuously being broken as the light boat twists and turns on the waves.

West Wight Charters of Lymington have a reasonable glass shark boat, the Dominator Class *Bacalao*, built by Senior Marine of Southampton. I had quite a lot to do with the lay-out of the deck area of this boat, and have used it to catch several big porbeagles from the Isle of Wight grounds. For a glass boat, the Dominator is comparatively heavy and because of this it sits well in a sea and tends to drift in an even line, without corkscrewing from side to side. Thirty-two feet in length, this particular boat provides a good fishing platform and plenty of cover for eight or ten people. The decks are uncluttered, giving plenty of room to bring shark inboard with the minimum amount of trouble. I think that in time the game fishing catamarans used in the Pacific and off the East African coasts will become standard shark-fishing boats in this country, but as yet few of these fine craft have been built for use in home waters.

In the case of all boats working offshore, safety equipment in the form of ship-to-shore radio, and direction finding equipment, etc, is absolutely essential. This is particularly true of shark boats, which either work a long way from the coast or in dangerous tidal races like those off St Catherine's Point on the Isle of Wight. In spite of this, there are still shark-boat skippers who put to sea, day after day, in boats which are totally devoid of these essentials. New Board of Trade regulations will no doubt change this situation by forcing skippers to install such equipment, and anglers should in my opinion do everything possible to ensure that they only charter boats which incorporate these basic essentials. Accidents can happen to the best of boats, and a radio transceiver or direction-finder can quickly turn from being a basic bit of electronic equipment to a lifesaver second to none.

Sharking is a rough, tough sport, demanding a great deal from boats and men alike, and the sooner skippers and anglers alike realize this and take as many precautions as possible, the better. Most charter-boat skippers are cautious, experienced men who have already taken note of all Board of Trade regulations, but there are still many who take small boats into dangerous places without basic safety equipment aboard. Anglers who sail with such skippers have only themselves to blame if they become endangered at sea. Anglers and skippers alike should take the trouble to check with port authorities at least once a season to see if the Board of Trade have drawn up any new rulings or amendments concerning safety requirements – and most years you will find that they have!

Owners having boats built should, in their own interests, have their new craft finished off to Board of Trade standards. This adds considerably to the overall initial cost of the boat but is cheaper in the long run. It will not be long now before port authorities are issued with orders to ensure that boats operating on charter-hire basis must comply with existing safety regulations. In many cases this may mean a complete refitting of a boat, and so it would pay to have the job done in the first place.

Rubby-Dubby

Although all British sharks show a marked reluctance to eat stale fish baits, they can be attracted to a boat by the smell and taste of rotting fish. All shark-boat skippers take advantage of this by using a revolting mixture known as rubby-dubby to draw the shark in towards the boat. The basic idea of rubby-dubby probably originated in America where shark and game fishermen have used minced fish as an attractor for many years. The early pioneers of British shark fishing adapted the American idea for use on blue shark in Cornish waters, since which time most anglers out for a day's shark fishing have used this form of groundbaiting as a standard method of enticing shark to their baits.

It is noticeable that rubby-dubby works best when used for blue or porbeagle shark. Makos and threshers occasionally show up in a rubby-dubby slick, but I personally have strong doubts as to whether either of these fish actually follow a scent trail in the same way as the other two species. Blues and porbeagles are essentially 'pack' sharks, living and feeding on a group basis.

Threshers and makos, on the other hand, are more inclined to hunt in pairs or singly, and I doubt that either species can be stimulated to a feeding frenzy by a scent trail comprised of fish scraps and pilchard oil. Pack sharks of the blue and porbeagle type are an entirely different proposition. Each shoal member must compete with its companions for food, and a scent trail – no matter how faint it may be – will bring the fish for miles in the hope of an easy meal.

When I have been out after blue shark in Cornish waters, I have seen fish come sniffing up to a rubby-dubby trail by the dozen, and on more than one occasion I and my companions have notched up catches of over twenty fish in a single day's fishing. Although seldom as plentiful as blues, porbeagles also have such moments. On the Isle of Wight grounds there are occasions when the whole area surrounding the boat seems to be jam-packed with fish. Usually when a big porbeagle pack turns up the individual weight of fish tends to run between 80 lb and 150 lb, but there are times when a smallish group of really big fish put in a surprise appearance. When this happens, one should look out for fireworks.

When pack shark develop a feeding frenzy they often tend to go on a wild rampage, showing a total lack of awareness of man or boat in the process. Time and again I have witnessed normally timid shark go on one of these sprees and I have always been amazed at their ferocity. Porbeagle are particularly bombastic and will repeatedly charge the rubby-dubby container in an attempt to get at the minced fish inside it. Several times I have had porbeagles tear the sack off the side of the boat, and they will then often snatch at a bait the moment it is lowered into the water. This behaviour can lead to some pretty exciting and highly spectacular fishing, of a kind normally only encountered in tropical seas.

I suppose every shark expert has his own favourite form of rubby-dubby and many a secret and highly offensive concoction has been tried out in the hope that it contains that little extra which no shark can hope to resist. Frankly, I have tried most of the more exotic recipes for making up rubby-dubby, but as yet I have still to discover anything better than a mixture comprised of mashed fish, bran, and pilchard oil. At a pinch, almost any kind of fish can be used to make up a rubby-dubby mix, but soft-fleshed oily fish, like mackerel, herring and pilchard make the best basic ingredient. Stale, smelly fish make much better rubby-dubby than fresh ones, and wherever possible I like to leave my rubby-dubby fish to ripen in the sun for at least a day before I use them. Stale fish are of course much easier to mince or mash and are naturally far more smelly than fresh ones. This is important, since in grinding the fish to paste before mixing it with bran and neat pilchard oil, one can arrive at a mixture which dispenses fairly easily from a finely meshed rubby-dubby bag.

I pay particular attention to making my first batches of rubby-dubby at the start of each day's fishing, as I consider it essential to begin operations with a really smooth, potent smell lane leading away from the boat. This forms the basis for the day's fishing. I am less fussy about keeping up such a high-quality slick later on in the day. This is simply because I am certain that once the initial trail has been laid, any shark that scents it will follow it back to source, providing that a steady stream of fish scraps, bran and oil continues to form an unbroken trail.

Quite a few anglers make up their rubby-dubby without including bran. This, I believe, is a great mistake, as bran quickly absorbs the oil and the moisture of the rubby-dubby, thereby helping to stiffen the mixture considerably. More important still, the wet bran sinks fairly rapidly and disperses easily in the water. This helps to broaden and deepen the trail, often bringing in shark which in the ordinary way would have been swimming too deep to pick up an ordinary surface trail. This is particularly true of porbeagles and to a lesser extent threshers, which often tend to sulk about close to the bottom. Blue shark are basically surface feeders, but even so I still think it advisable to use bran when rubby-dubbing for any species. Some anglers try to save money by using fine sawdust in place of bran. However, since sawdust invariably has a strong smell, I believe it tends to repel rather than attract all types of shark.

As I said earlier, soft, oily-fleshed fish make the best basic ingredient for a rubby-dubby mix. At a pinch, however, it is quite possible to press other fish into service, and at one time or another I have caught sharks in scent trails made up from all sorts of weird and wonderful fish. Blood is said to be a great shark attractor, but my own experiences have shown that most animal bloods are useless for shark fishing. I have tried both chicken blood and ox blood, finally coming to the conclusion that I was wasting my time in this direction, and I have never bothered to pursue the subject further. Fish blood, particularly shark blood, is a very good attractor indeed and I have noticed that on many occasions when I have had a badly gaffed shark strapped alongside the boat, the constant drip of fresh blood from the corpse seems to drive other shark wild. Shark or tope livers, minced and mixed in with the basic rubby-dubby mix, also add to the attractiveness of the scent trail. This is particularly true when porbeagles are the quarry, although blues also seem to respond well.

When using minced shark liver, mixed with mashed fish, pilchard oil and bran, I have had several encounters with shark which have attempted to drag the rubby-dubby bag off the side of the boat. Normally I hang it over the side so that roughly a third of it is submerged, and the constant rise and fall of the boat on the waves then continuously lifts it clear of the water before smacking it back on to the surface. This constant movement activates the contents of the bag, ensuring a continuous stream of rubby-dubby particles drifting away on the tide. At ten- or fifteen-minute intervals I give the bag a really good shake-up for good measure, and more often than not add a handful or two to freshen it up. I usually perform this shaking-up function by pulling the bag out of the water by its cord and banging it up and down on the surface for a minute or two, keeping my eyes on the balloon floats rather than on the bait sack.

On more than one occasion, however, I have picked up the cord with the intention of giving the sack a shake and found that a shark has beaten me to it and is hanging grimly on to the other end. Once I even had a porbeagle lunge up out of the water and take the bag in the air. On many occasions I have seen the fish come sweeping in for an attack on the bag and have only just managed to lift it out of the water in time. These incidents, although interesting from the spectactor angle, can be a perfect nuisance – once a shark sets its mind on getting the rubby-dubby sack, nothing short of catching the fish will stop it.

Fortunately, sharks that try for the sack will usually snatch at anything edible that comes their way and a favourite trick of mine is to lift the sack at the exact second that someone drops a baited hook in its place. The hungry shark, intent only on food, will usually suck this in without any preliminary investigation whatsoever. This sort of fishing has terrific visual impact which adds considerably to the overall excitement of shark fishing. Fortunately, it does not happen often enough to become boring. I suppose a dozen or so times a season the shark go on to feed in this way, and each time it happens I am impressed by the fish's total lack of fear of either the boat or the men in it. It is at times like this that I would not like to fall into the water, for under these circumstances I am fairly certain in my own mind that there would be every possibility of attack.

At one time or another I have tried a wide variety of containers, but these days I simply use a finely meshed vegetable sack of the type greengrocers use for onions or carrots. These are easily obtainable in quantity, work well at sea, and can be discarded at the end of the day. A thin cord threaded through the neck of one of these mesh bags acts as a neat draw-string, keeping the bag closed when in the water yet easy to open when fresh rubby-dubby is required. The positioning of the rubby-dubby bag on a boat is a matter of personal preference. I like mine to hang from the middle section of the boat on the side from which I am fishing. Other anglers prefer it at the bow or stern, and if the truth were known it does not really matter so long as a constant flow of rubby-dubby seeps away with the tide. In rough weather, when the shark tend to swim deeper than normal, I usually put the rubby sack out on the opposite side of the boat so that the bait trail hits the side and hull of the boat and sinks quickly. I believe that this helps to bring in shark which would have missed a surface scent trail completely.

One thing is for certain: rubby-dubby is vital and to catch fish consistently it is essential to maintain a constant smell trail at all times. Neglect to do this and you may as well not bother to fish, for unless you are lucky enough to drift over shark by accident your chances of success are non-existent. Believe me, it is impossible to over-emphasize the importance of rubby-dubby. It is better to go out short of fresh bait than to go with inferior supplies of groundbait. Rubby-dubby also attracts fish other than sharks, and there have been times when I have seen the water round the boat so thick with mackerel that each wave which broke seemed to consist of fish rather than water. This, of course, makes for excellent hunting, for if you can attract and hold the bait-fish shoals close to the boat, the combined efforts of the rubby-dubby trail and splashing bait fish will soon bring the shark nosing in. Time and again I have seen the shoaling mackerel rush to get under the boat, and at exactly that second one of my shark reels has started to sing out. Indeed, I have never come back fishless when the rubby-dubby has brought in the bait fish.

Bait

Size and choice of bait depends a great deal on where you

intend to fish and which species of shark you hope to catch. The most widely used bait of all is mackerel, mainly because it is usually easy to obtain fresh and in quantity, and also because all shark seem to find it acceptable as food. In West-Country waters, mackerel accounts for well over ninety per cent of the annual blue-shark catches, while elsewhere it accounts for por-beagle, thresher and mako. Good as it is, there are occasions when I am sure other baits would produce better results. Por-beagle shark, for example, spend a great deal of time scouting about over sunken rocks and submerged reefs, feeding for the main part on rock-haunting fish like pollack, pouting, coalfish and possibly wrasse. At these times I am quite convinced that a large pollack or big pout would attract far more shark than a mackerel.

It is difficult to convince anglers of this fact, however. Having caught shark on shiny mackerel baits they have no confidence in other bait fish, despite the fact that a careful examination of the stomach contents of shark usually shows a high predominance of rock fish, which proves that not only will the shark eat such fish but in all probability they prefer them to mackerel. Over the years I have kept fairly detailed records of the sharks I have either caught myself or have been involved in catching, and the baits that were used. These records show that at one time or another I have caught shark on mackerel, pil-chard, garfish, squid, pollack, coalfish, pouting, herring, whiting and wrasse. Pollack and pout have accounted for many of the larger fish, and I know that West-Country anglers who fish for mako generally like to use a 2–3 lb pollack as bait. This is logical when you realize that makos tend to hang about up-jutting rocks like the Manacles or the Eddystone Reef, where pollack are very common indeed.

Contrary to popular belief, shark are not dirty feeders and unless a bait is very fresh indeed they are unlikely to pay it much attention. There are of course exceptions to every rule, and I know of several outstanding instances of very big shark falling to stinking baits. A 299½ lb porbeagle, caught at the end of the 1970 Isle of Wight season, fell to a very 'niffy' herring, and the present record mako was induced to strike at a chunk of rotten mackerel. These instances are exceptional, however, and my advice to anyone going sharking is to obtain the freshest bait possible, and to try to catch even more fresh bait during actual fishing time.

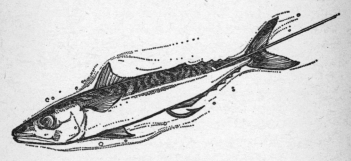

Live-bait hooked through root of tail

In their natural state, shark are active predators rather than offal eaters. Because of this I like to use live baits whenever possible. Live-baiting is undoubtedly a cruel method of ang- ling, although nature is just as cruel in its own way. I myself have no qualms about impaling a live fish on a big hook, but many anglers cannot bring themselves to do so. To keep a bait alive on the hook, I find there is only one method of baiting up that really works. This is to pass the hook point and barb right through the bait's body, some two or three inches before the root of its tail. The fish can then hang freely from the bend of the hook. A bait hooked like this can flap about clumsily, and must look to the shark like a sick or badly damaged fish and therefore an easy meal. Like all predatory creatures, shark are quick to take advantage of any easy meal they come across, and because of this I find my live-baits catch far more fish than dead-baits of similar size fished in a similar fashion. Live-baits can also be used to encourage a timid or lethargic shark. On many occasions when a shark has continually refused to look at a dead-bait, I have managed to catch it by using a live fish.

If for one reason or another live-baits are impossible to obtain, I try to play on the shark's naturally greedy nature by using very big dead-baits. In common with all big fish, shark are naturally lazy creatures, and if they can get one big meal instead of chasing about for a number of small ones, they will invariably settle for it. Large dead-baits are not always readily available, and more often than not I am forced to use two bait fish, mounted tandem fashion, one slightly above the other. This double bait looks totally unnatural in the water, but as it catches fish its appearance does not really seem to matter too much. When I am able to get big dead-baits easily, I usually attach them to the trace and hook in the following way. First the hook is threaded through the root of the bait's tail and right out through its body. The trace is then wound once round the bait and the hook is passed up through its gill slit and out through its mouth. The whole of the hook, with the exception of the point and barb, is now hidden inside the bait, where it will not alarm a taking fish.

Readers will notice that I always arrange my baits to hang head downwards on the hook. This is because all predatory fish, including shark, swallow their food head foremost. Thus, when I strike at a running shark, the chances are that the head of the bait and the protruding hook will be far enough inside its mouth or gullet for the hook to engage in solid flesh. Live-baits are a different proposition entirely, since in order to keep a bait alive and in fairly good condition the only possible place to position the hook is at the tail-end of the bait's body, where it will cause no damage to the gills or other vital organs. With only one hook-hold at this extremity, there is of course a chance of missing a shark on the strike. Fortunately, shark seem to approach live-bait with such confidence that they rarely run off with one without immediately starting to swallow it.

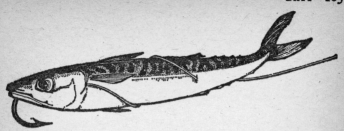

Dead-bait hooked with trace wound round body

Baiting up in these ways will accommodate most standard techniques of shark fishing. When trolling for shark, however, a different method should be used, and this is described on page 124–5.

. . . and How to Use It

Fishing from a Drifting Boat
Float-fishing
Free-lining
Legering
Fishing from an Anchored Boat
Trolling
Finishing them off

Fishing from a Drifting Boat

Shark fishing has been widely practised in West-Country waters for at least twenty years. During this time thousands of shark have been caught and thousands of anglers have been initiated into the sport. In recent years, however, the cult of shark hunting has begun to spread and anglers all along the Channel coast are now taking an active interest in trying to develop the fishing in hitherto untried areas. The now famous Isle of Wight grounds are a typical example of a new fishing area being discovered and developed, and it looks as though similar fisheries at Weymouth and Newhaven will soon be in full operation. Because of all this activity and interest, it seems strange to me that there is as yet only one recognized method of shark fishing. I refer, of course, to the technique of fishing from a drifting boat, using a rubby-dubby bag to attract the foraging shark to the angler's bait.

A drifting boat is dictated to by both wind and tide, and thus it pays to understand fully what effects these factors are likely to have on both the angle of drift and the actual trail of bait particles and oil from the rubby-dubby bag. Any drifting boat will be carried down tide with the movement of water, but the presence or absence of wind can make a great deal of difference to the effectiveness of the rubby-dubby slick. Ideally, the wind should be behind the boat so that the slick drifts squarely along on the tide run. More often than not, however, it is ruined by a prevailing cross wind which tends to push the boat at an angle across the actual run of tide. Many West-Country anglers are lucky enough to be able to fish an area where even full spring tides are slack in comparison to the strength of those encountered off the St Catherine's end of the Isle of Wight. Shark boats working in the vicinity of Looe, Mevagissey, and Fowey have the best of the tides, of course, which begin to pick up again in earnest further down at Falmouth.

Probably the worst possible combination for shark fishing on the drift is on a full neap tide when there is no wind whatsoever to push the boat along. Under these circumstances, the rubby-dubby trail simply sinks beneath the boat and one's chances of attracting fish become virtually non-existent. Under conditions of this kind, luck is the only thing that can bring a fish. With wind and tide together, the boat will usually drift well and the resulting rubby-dubby trail can be seen floating away for a considerable distance in front of the baits. Under these circumstances, I always feel completely confident of catching a fish or two, and I am usually lucky. Shark are restless, nomadic fish which are forced by nature to keep on the move or drown. Consequently, a drifting boat which covers a considerable area of water stands a good chance of finding a few fish. I do not feel that drifting is always the answer, however, and later in this section I will discuss fishing from an anchored boat. As yet, this is rarely practised by British shark fishermen, although in other parts of the world it is a recognized technique, bringing in plenty of very big fish.

Float-fishing

Float-fishing is the most widely recognized method of taking shark in British waters and there can be little doubt that it is a highly effective method of angling. Where I fish, few boats work more than three sets of tackle at a time, although in the West Country, boats specializing in hunting blues regularly fish six rods side by side. This in my opinion is bad practice, as when a shark is hooked, tangled lines are an absolute certainty, leading to the loss of valuable fishing time. I much prefer to fish with only the three sets of tackle, so that the moment a run occurs the other two anglers can get their lines inboard and out of the way, leaving the lucky angler a clear field in which to play and beat his fish.

Probably the most difficult thing about float fishing for shark is trying to decide at which depth the fish will be inclined to feed on each given day. As far as I can see, there are no fixed rules about this. Sometimes the shark can be located deep down close to the sea bed, while on other occasions they will be found in a feeding mood just under the surface. At the start of each day's fishing, it is anybody's guess as to where they may be, although as an all-round taking depth, I find I catch most fish on baits worked at 30–40 feet below the surface. With three rods out, it is advisable to set each outfit at a different depth, for example at 4, 6, and 10 fathoms. In this way, a wide range of depths can be covered and, if there are any fish about, it will not be long before one shows up on one of the baits. The remaining two sets of gear can then be altered accordingly. I give these three settings as a basis on which to begin operations, but one should remember that there are no hard and fast rules in angling, and shark fishing is no exception. It is always worthwhile experimenting should these particular depths produce no response.

Only recently I was down for a day's blue-shark fishing off Mevagissey in Cornwall. Although in all I caught seven sharks,

I had to change depths continually throughout the day in order to keep track of the fish as they changed their feeding levels. Several of the blues I caught that day were hooked at depths exceeding 100 feet, while other fish were taken at less than 10 feet below the surface. A fairly good guide to the most likely depth of the shark is to locate the mackerel shoals by feathering a few strings of fish for fresh bait. Most shark rely on shoaling mackerel to provide them with an easy supply of food, and if the mackerel are found to be shoaling at, say, 40 feet below the surface, it is quite likely that the shark will be patrolling and feeding at a similar depth. Again, one should not assume that shoaling mackerel remain at a constant level throughout the day, and from time to time it pays to use the feathers to establish their exact whereabouts. Any significant change of depth can then be allowed for by a readjustment of tackle.

Despite being rather stupid fish, shark of all kinds show an inbred cunning which can make them extremely difficult to catch. When they are in a mad feeding spasm, they will snatch at anything edible that crosses their path, but under normal circumstances they are quick to take fright and will drop a suspect bait at the slightest indication of danger. I am sure that the major reason for fish taking alarm during the initial stages of a run is purely and simply the size and buoyancy of the float being used. So many anglers assume that fish as large and as voracious as shark totally ignore the drag imposed by a float. This is entirely wrong, and to catch shark in consistent quantities it is essential to use as small and as streamlined a float as will support the bait in the water.

Cornish shark-men rely on flat crab-pot corks for their floats, whereas the Southern Irish shark-boat skippers usually plump for a plastic detergent bottle. In my opinion, neither are ideal, although at a pinch both can be used fairly successfully. For porbeagle hunting on the Isle of Wight grounds, partially inflated party balloons are the most widely used floats, but even with these great care should be taken to ensure that they do not create too much drag on the surface. I normally blow my balloons up to a little over the size of a large orange. At this stage the balloon will support two whole mackerel and the weight of the steel trace while offering little or no resistance to a biting shark.

Basically, there are two effective ways of attaching a balloon to the reel line. The simplest is to measure off the required

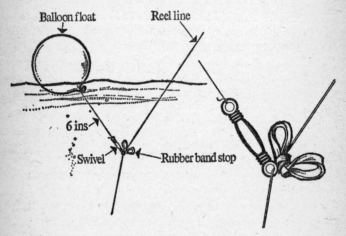

Sliding link float attachment

distance between bait and float, and tie the balloon to the actual reel line with a length of fine sewing cotton. In this way, the balloon float is securely attached to the line, yet free to break away the moment the shark picks up the bait and dives. Obviously one loses a balloon on each bite, but this is a small price to pay for the fish one catches. This crude but highly efficient break-away rig allows the fish to move off on a free line, leading to very few losses through the fish ejecting a bait.

The angler who likes to preserve his balloon float should use the sliding link attachment. This simply consists of a short length of line tied directly to the neck of the balloon, to the loose end of which is attached a small barrel swivel. When the tackle is set up in the first place, the reel line should be threaded through the open eye of the swivel before the trace is attached. Once this is done the swivel, link and balloon are free to slide up or down the reel line. A rubber band hitched to the reel line acts as a stop for the swivel. This stop can be attached at whatever depth is required, and can be easily altered at will, so that the bait can be fished higher or lower in the water as circumstances dictate. The main drawback to this neat and efficient sliding attachment is that the balloon must remain fixed to the line at all times. Consequently the biting shark does stand the chance of feeling the drag of the float. To compensate for this, I find it advisable to cut the size of the inflated balloon to the absolute minimum. Using elongated rather than round balloons will also help to minimize the danger of float-drag disturbing the shark.

Being rather a fanatical shark angler, I like to take every precaution possible to avoid alarming a biting fish, and because of this I seldom – if ever – stray far from my rod. At the first sign of a bite, my standard practice is to pick up the rod so that the tip points directly at the float, at the same time throwing the ratchet mechanism on the reel out of gear, using my thumb as a reel brake. By doing this at the first sign of a bite, I am in a position to give line to a running fish with the absolute minimum amount of drag. I feel this is of vital importance, although I know many anglers who do not bother to pick up the rod until a shark has run off a fair amount of line against the drag of a ratchet. These same anglers are inclined to laugh at my style of angling, since in their opinion I credit shark with a power of reasoning which they do not actually possess. I can see their point of view but at the same time my record of successful runs is very, very high indeed, which leads me to believe that I am in fact on the right track.

During periods of bad weather, shark will sometimes pick up a bait and chew it to rags without causing the float to give any clear indication of a bite. Small porbeagle shark are particularly prone to this exasperating form of behaviour. How they do it is beyond me, but time and again I have retrieved my tackle to find either that the bait has gone completely, or that it has been chopped in half or chewed beyond recognition. To lose bait after bait in this way can be very frustrating, and to try to overcome this hazard I have formed the habit of holding the rod whenever I fish shark in a rough sea. In this way, I have managed to catch quite a few of these nibblers, which in all probability I would never have hooked if I had left the rod to fish for itself in the standard shark-fishing manner. It is amazing just how sensitive a rod can be. It may be difficult at first to determine whether wave action or a biting shark is responsible for each pull at the rod tip, but one can soon become sufficiently accustomed to each kind of movement to be able to recognize just when a shark is beginning to mouth at the bait.

I find most of these nibble bites are registered on the rod tip as a series of slow but definitely hard pulls. Normally, when I feel this series of movements through the rod, I throw the reel out of gear and free spool a yard or two of line back to the fish. This seems to encourage the shark to greater efforts and often a full-blooded run develops within seconds of the fish getting slack line. If a proper run does occur, it can be dealt with in the normal way. On the other hand, some shark will not fall for this tactic and continue to pick up and drop the bait as though hesitant to feed properly. This behaviour can put the angler in a difficult position, since if he leaves the fish to play with the bait for any length of time, it will either succeed in removing the bait from the hook or it will simply lose interest and move off. To overcome this lethargy on the part of the shark, I find it pays to annoy it by deliberately pulling the bait away. A long slow backward sweep with the rod tip will achieve this, and by repeating the process two or three times the fish can usually be induced to make a determined rush at the bait.

Shark of all kinds can be forced into action by these tactics, and a disinterested fish can be turned into a feeding fish in a few moments. These finicky shark really have to be handled with kid gloves, however. Even though they may have been teased into taking the bait properly, they will not stand any nonsense and will drop it again at the slightest sign of trouble. Once again, it pays to put the reel into the free-spool position, so that the fish can take off against the minimum amount of rod and reel drag. One should not delay the strike any longer than is absolutely essential, for a fish which is already disinclined to feed properly is likely to jettison the bait and hook at the slightest excuse.

I have a theory that most shark, and in particular porbeagle, like a bait that moves. Fish are obviously used to hunting and eating live food, and a stiff dead bait which just hangs in the water must appear very unnatural to them, in many ways. To try to give a bait more shark appeal, I have formed the habit of keeping it on the move, simply by winding it in and then letting it out again to its original position. By doing this at half-hourly intervals, I find I pick up quite a number of shark which I am quite convinced I would not catch if I let my bait out in the normal way. I am fairly certain that at times big shark will shadow a bait for long periods without making any attempt whatsoever to take it. They are presumably puzzled by its lack of movement and, not being particularly hungry, are content just to keep an eye on the fish while trying to make up their minds what to do about it. If, however, the semi-static bait suddenly begins to sidle off, the trailing shark often charges straight at it on a sort of reflex-action basis.

I find that when I draw a bait back to the boat, I get a high percentage of strikes within a few yards of the boat's sides. Occasionally a fish will hit the bait as it runs back out to its original position, but it normally bites on the retrieve. Very often I am close enough to the bait to get a clear view of the shark as it charges in to the attack. At this stage it is essential to keep a clear head and to continue retrieving at the same steady speed. To slow down the rate of retrieve, or to stop it entirely, usually makes the shark swerve off-course, deliberately by-passing the bait. The shark obviously sees the bait as a live fish and expects it to take avoiding action and not to slow down. Thus, if you see a shark following right behind, it is essential to keep the bait moving at all costs.

Free-lining

There is something very pleasant about float fishing for shark, particularly when the sea is rather flat and still, and every movement of the float can be clearly seen. Float fishing is not, however, the begin-all and end-all of shark fishing, and al-though most anglers have yet to catch a fish by any other method, I personally feel that in time many will discard the float in favour of the free-line technique. Contrary to popular belief, a float is not really a bite indicator, although it can obviously be used as such. Strictly speaking, however, its main purpose is to support the bait at a given depth in the water. There are days when for one reason or another float fishing is not a practical proposition, and at these times I turn to free-lining with every confidence of catching fish.

Free-lining, as its name implies, is a technique which allows the bait to drop freely down through the water. The angler can stop the bait at any given depth simply by putting the reel on the rachet or by using his thumb as a brake on the line. I have used the free-lining method a great deal for blue shark off the south coast of Cornwall, and to a lesser extent for porbeagles off the Isle of Wight. In both areas, this technique has produced plenty of fish, usually on really rough days when normal float fishing would be difficult.

The beauty of the free-line method is that in very rough water the bait can be sent down to a preselected depth where it will fish on a fairly even keel. A similar bait, fished in similar conditions but suspended beneath a buoyant balloon, would rise and fall at a terrific rate as the balloon bobbed about on the waves. Naturally enough, the boat will rise and fall the same as the balloon, but by holding the rod and raising or lowering the tip to compensate for the movement of the waves, one can fish the bait so that it remains fairly stable at all times. The free-lining technique can also be used to fish a bait down close to the sea-bed, since the weight of a good-sized mackerel is usually more than enough to take the tackle right down to this level. On those occasions when the shark are feeding right on, or very close to the bottom, float fishing can be very awkward, and nowadays I rely entirely on the free line for this deep-water sharking.

Legering

Some shark, particularly threshers and porbeagles, are inclined to spend a fair amount of time bottom feeding. At present few anglers attempt to catch fish under these circumstances, although I am sure that in time legering will become a standard shark-fishing technique. Legering is a static form of angling, best practised from an anchored boat. Nothing special is really required for this method of fishing – just a suitably sized lead to hold the terminal tackle down on the bottom. Standard-length shark traces should be used, the lead being allowed to slide on the reel line. A boatman friend of mine at Weymouth has hooked a number of very big porbeagle shark while bottom fishing over mixed ground for conger and skate, and in Christchurch Bay many good-sized threshers have been hooked, boated, or lost, by anglers legering for tope over a bottom comprised of sand and shingle. There are tremendous possibilities for development along these lines, but as yet legering is a practically untouched field of shark fishing.

I remember some years ago taking a party of anglers out to a deep hole situated some miles south of the Needles Lighthouse. On this particular day we were out in search of skate and tope, and as the hole looked a likely place for fish of this type we decided to brave the strong tides and try to fish directly into the centre of the hole itself. After steaming out the required distance, it was not long before the echo-sounder picked up the inside edge of the hole we were looking for. A few minutes later, down went the first baits into practically virgin water. Almost immediately, a good thornback was brought to the gaff and for a while everyone aboard was kept busy with small and medium-sized skate. Then, quite abruptly everything went dead, and it looked as though our sport was over.

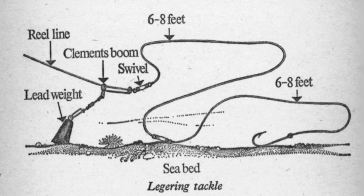

Legering tackle

Suddenly, one of the stern rods slammed over in two incredible jags as something large snatched at the bait. The angler holding the rod played safe and let the fish pull at the bait again before attempting to set the hook. In fact, when the second stage of the bite came there was no point in striking; the big boat rod simply bent into a most impressive half-circle as whatever was on the other end engulfed the bait and took off. There was nothing very spectacular about the run, except for the fact that the angler could do nothing to stop its progress. The fish had no great speed; it simply ploughed steadily away from the boat, dragging yard after yard of line after it. Naturally enough, the angler tried everything he knew to try to slow the fish down and turn it far enough to be able to control it, but despite heavy rod pressure it went steadily on until every inch of line was off the reel. Then with a *ping*, the knot holding the line to the reel spool parted and the fish was gone.

Twice more, within the space of half an hour, the same process was repeated. Finally, when a fourth run resulted in a smashed rod, one of the anglers set up some really heavy tackle, baited his 10–0 hook with a whole mackerel, and sent his leger down to the bottom in the hope that his bait would be found by one of the unknown monsters. At this stage I was inclined to think the fish responsible for smashing the tackle were big skate, as at this time no one had thought about shark fishing in the area. Thus, shark were far from our minds when the next bite came. Again the rod wagged twice, and the fish began to cruise slowly away. The angler, fully confident of the strength of his tackle, struck hard in an attempt to fluster the fish into making a mistake. In actual fact it was the angler who made the mistake, for the moment he struck, the fish on the other end of his line stopped ambling about, shifted into top gear, and went off at almost incredible speed.

From the angle of the line, I could see the fish was coming up and right away I dismissed the skate theory from my mind. No skate could swim as fast as this fish, nor for that matter would a skate run up towards the surface. Tope just did not have this kind of strength, and so it could only be shark. Indeed, shark it was, and a big one at that. It came straight up out of the water, stood on its great tail and fell back on the line with a tremendous crash. No line can take this sort of punishment and this one was no exception. It parted like cotton under the savage impact and the fish was gone.

We did not get another shark bite during the remainder of the day, but with broken lines and a smashed rod to show for our troubles we had certainly experienced some exciting fishing. Most important of all was the fact that each shark had been hooked on the bottom with a basic leger rig. At the time this did not seem to matter, but looking back on the incident after some pretty busy shark-fishing seasons I am sure that legering could well be a top method. Without a shadow of doubt, the shark we hooked that day were porbeagles and, if the one that jumped was anything to go by, pretty big ones at that. Legering is a practically untouched method of shark fishing, and until I have the opportunity to give this technique a more thorough testing, it is difficult to draw any conclusions as to is overall effectiveness. However, in the light of my experience, and that of the Weymouth boatman, it could easily prove to be a winner if fully developed.

Fishing from an Anchored Boat

At least ninety-eight per cent of the shark caught round the British Isles are caught from boats drifting with the tide. This has long been the accepted technique and most shark-boat skippers adhere to it rigidly. West-country boats working blue shark never attempt to anchor, and sharkers working other areas have all tended to follow suit. This is quite understandable, since a drifting boat spreads a long wide slick and covers a great deal of ground during the course of a day's fishing. With free-swimming shark like blues and makos, this is the obvious technique to employ, but when porbeagle and possibly thresher shark are the quarry, a new school of thought suggests that anchoring could bring more and bigger fish.

The main reason for supposing this is that porbeagle tend to be a rather residential species, content to stay in one particular locality for long periods of time, instead of ranging far and wide in search of food. I know from my own shark catches on the Isle of Wight grounds that certain well-defined areas are more productive than others, and because of this most shark-boat skippers working off the Island try to angle their line of drift so that their boats pass right through the known hot-spots.

These tactics produce at least sixty per cent of the fish caught off the Island each season and it has now reached the stage where anglers and skippers alike know just when they stand the best chance of hooking or sighting a fish.

There are no hard and fast rules in angling, but with porbeagle it is in fact almost possible to foretell where and when one can expect to make contact. Weymouth boatman Tony Pearce accidentally located a hot-spot of this kind during the 1971 season, when to his great surprise he found that anglers bottom-fishing with big baits were hooking and losing big shark three or four times a week. He finally decided to hang a shark line over the stern in an attempt to pick up one of the marauders. The result was a superb fish of 187 lb, hooked on a single mackerel bait. It fought for nearly an hour before it could be brought to gaff, and was the first big porbeagle ever caught in recent years by an angler fishing from an anchored boat.

Shark fishing at anchor has several distinct disadvantages. The strong tidal areas frequented by porbeagles can really only accommodate this technique during neap tides or slack-water periods, since the force of the tide flow would otherwise lift the mackerel bait right up to the surface, where it may be missed by a hungry shark. It may be possible to overcome this problem by using additional lead to weigh the bait down, but as yet no one has attempted to try out this technique. The most notable disadvantage, however, is the likelihood of a hooked fish running up tide and fouling the reel line or trace around the anchor rope. This could be avoided by slipping the anchor on to a buoy line the moment a fish is hooked. This would allow the boat to drift away from the anchor rope, so that the fish could be played out in the conventional manner. When it has been brought inboard and dispatched, the boat could be motored back to the buoyed anchor line and made fast, and out could go the shark lines once more.

As in drift fishing, rubby-dubby still plays an important part when sharking from an anchored boat. Tony Pearce, for example, keeps up a steady flow of chopped mackerel, so that a stream of bait continually works away with the tide to attract and hold the attention of any sharks which happen to be in the vicinity. At present, he does not attempt to use a rubby-dubby bag as well, but I would be inclined to use both bag and chopped fish to lay the scent trail. The bag could be attached either to the eye-hole of the marker buoy or to the rope directly beneath it. This would ensure that the rubby-dubby trail would continue to flow even when the boat was a mile or more away from its original position.

This style of shark fishing is as yet only in its infancy. However, Tony Pearce has already proved that it works, and no doubt next season anchoring for shark will become a recognized and highly productive technique. Not all porbeagle hot-spots are in areas where anchoring is possible. But with those that are, the obvious advantages of going directly to a mark which is a known haunt of big shark, and fishing on it for a whole day, outweigh the disadvantages of having to slip anchor each time a fish is hooked. I hope that in future seasons one or two of the Isle of Wight shark marks can be fished in this manner.

Although drift fishing from a moving boat can be highly productive, really top-notch marks are often covered in a remarkably short space of time by fishing from a stationary boat placed right over the middle of such an area. By keeping up a steady trail of bait particles, it should be possible to draw the bulk of the shark population to the boat and pick them off one by one. Travelling fish drifting in with each new tide should help to replenish stocks of residential shark and, with a little conservation on the angler's part, a good mark should continue to provide sport throughout the season.

Trolling

Very little constructive trolling has ever been done in English waters, although various techniques are used extensively abroad, for game fish such as tuna, swordfish, and certain species of surface-feeding shark. During the 1970 shark season, I carried out experiments with trolling tackle on the Isle of Wight shark grounds, while Kevin Linhane of the Irish Tourist Board carried out similar experiments off Achill Island. In both widely separated areas, we found that porbeagle reacted favourably to trolled baits, but as yet we are unable to discover whether this technique can be really effective with the other species of British shark.

Any angler who wishes to try his hand at the art of trolling would be well advised to fish an area noted for porbeagles. From my own experience in this field, I am inclined to believe that trolled baits normally attract the smaller fish. Although I have caught porbeagle weighing up to exactly 170 lb while trolling, the average fish I catch weighs considerably less than this. In Ireland the same thing seems to apply. The bulk of the porbeagle caught while trolling around the Achill Island area have been good but not outstanding fish, tipping the scales at 100–125 lb. It could be of course that the smaller fish are more plentiful and more active than the really big chaps, and therefore by the law of averages more likely to be caught. However, I think that time will in fact show that porbeagle above a certain size have a tendency to change their habits, preferring to pick up an easy meal rather than hunting actively for their food. Big fish of all kinds are lazy creatures and very big porbeagle are no exception to this rule. This theory is backed up by the fact that smallish porbeagles are often very active on the surface, whereas the very large fish seldom put in a surface appearance.

In New Zealand, where hunting makos is an extremely popular sport, trolling is the only technique employed. The baits, which are very carefully prepared, are almost invariably natural, although artificial wooden teasers are also used to attract the shark. In English waters, of course, mako are by no means prolific and it is virtually impossible to go out deliberately trolling for them. Thus, when a mako is sighted most boats are equipped only with standard sharking equipment, and consequently every specimen caught off the Cornish coasts has been taken on a float-fished bait. As I said earlier, the ideal shark for trolling purposes is the porbeagle, which is extremely common in many areas, and is inclined by nature to give chase to a bait which moves across its line of vision. So far, all the porbeagles I have caught while trolling have fallen to natural baits mounted on a special trolling rig. They also show definite interest in artificial lures, however, and I have known quite large specimens snap at minute baits like mackerel flies or mackerel spinners.

Jack Shine, the Irish expert, has frequently hooked hefty porbeagle on artificial mackerel lures, while fishing from the rocks at Green Island. On the Isle of Wight grounds similar encounters occur each season and many regular local fishermen can relate stories of shark striking at small artificial lures. During the 1970 season, quite a number of thresher shark were hooked off the Needles Lighthouse area by anglers using mackerel feathers, and in nearly all cases the fish cleared the water a number of times before breaking free of the tackle. Beach anglers feathering off Chesil Beach in Dorset also occasionally hook porbeagle on feathers, which is living proof that it might well pay to try some serious trolling with large artificial plugs or squid, in areas where porbeagles are thought to exist in fair quantities. I have a number of large tuna lures which I intend to experiment with in future seasons.

Movement of any kind seems to attract porbeagle shark, and many anglers who are playing a medium-sized bottom fish suddenly find that their catch has been taken or attacked by a marauding porbeagle. These sudden attacks usually result in the angler's fish being either torn right off the hook, or totally mangled. Bournemouth angler Derek Case experienced such an incident when cod fishing from Boscombe Pier. He had hooked a good cod and practically played it out, when a shark struck at it. The shark apparently grabbed the cod across the body, for all Derek managed to salvage was its head. The remainder of its body had been ripped right away. The cod's weight had been estimated at 14 lb, which is a fair indication of how large a fish a shark will attack.

In August of 1969, a boat angler fishing deep water behind the famed Shambles Bank hooked a good skate, played it half-way to the boat, and then had it taken by a shark which ran off over 100 yards of line before releasing the fish. Twice more it took the skate and let it go again, and when the fish was being brought to the gaff, the shark finally surged alongside and seized the fish by one wing. With less than ten feet of line between boat and shark the angler concerned could do little more than pull as hard as he dared in his attempts to make the shark drop his fish. Eventually, the shark tore away a substantial section of the skate's right wing and departed, leaving the angler to pull in just over half of his fish. During the time the shark had been alongside the boat, the angler and the skipper had seen it clearly and had both positively identified it as a porbeagle, and a big one at that, estimated at well over 200 lb in weight. This was a most significant sighting indeed, as it proved conclusively that porbeagle do in fact frequent the area around Portland Race.

I am so convinced that moving baits are highly attractive to porbeagle that, even when drifting with conventional shark fishing tackle, I make a habit of slowly winding the bait in towards the boat at regular intervals. If a bite does not occur during this winding-in process, I simply throw the reel into free spool and allow the bait to trot back out to its original position. I find this moving-bait tactic pays off consistently, and many of the big porbeagles I have caught in recent seasons have fallen to baits worked in this way. Most of the porbeagles caught by trolling off Southern Ireland have fallen to baits fished on lightly loaded tackle incorporating special two-hook rigs, trolled at one to two knots. The moment the fish takes the bait, the boatman throws the boat out of gear while the angler gives the taking fish as much free line as it requires.

Obviously, the way the bait behaves in the water is of prime importance when trolling. Because of this, great care must be taken to mount the bait correctly on the trolling trace. The two-hook trolling mount is constructed of stainless-steel wire. Hinged in the middle, the mount is made up in two sections, which gives flexibility to the bait. Two-hook rigs give a far greater hooking power than single-hook tackle, but by the same token they are twice as difficult to remove, and so many anglers may prefer to use a single-hook mount. This again is made from stainless-steel wire, a robust material which can be bought from most tackle dealers.

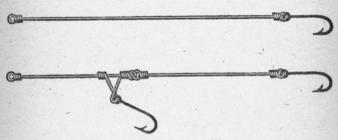

Single- and double-hook trolling mounts

Any trolling bait should work realistically in the water, and consequently to get the best action out of a bait the entire back-bone should be removed. The simplest way of doing this is to slit the bait from the tail to a point just behind the gill case. The backbone can then be removed easily, leaving the boneless bait intact. The hook trace should be pushed through the bait from the rear, so that the hook fits snugly along its belly. To stop the bait from pushing back on the trace, the lips should be stitched up with fine copper wire which can then be wound neatly round the protruding section of hook trace in order to hold it fast. A bait which is trolled with its mouth open will

quickly build up water pressure and begin to swerve erratically
from side to side in an unnatural fashion. It will also soon start
to break up and a ragged bait will seldom interest a shark.

Mackerel or horse mackerel make the best trolling baits.
Both are easy to obtain, clean to use and extremely streamlined.
Other more bulky fish make trolling difficult and should not be
used. To give additional weight, a two-ounce barrel can be

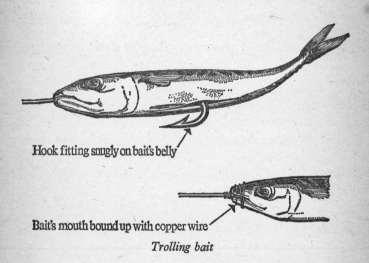

Hook fitting snugly on bait's belly

Bait's mouth bound up with copper wire

Trolling bait

pushed into the bait's mouth before it is sewn up. The commercial shark fishermen of Japan use an attractor device when
trolling for surface shark. This is called a 'Shava-shava' and is
designed to splash over the surface simulating the movements of
a small shoal of panic-stricken bait fish. I have recently obtained one of these devices, which in appearance resembles
nothing more than a winged coat hanger, and hope to use it for
porbeagle shark.

Trolling can only be carried out successfully in boats that
have a wide transom, and even then it is only possible for two

anglers to fish. This is of course a drawback, as few anglers other than those who are fortunate enough to own their own craft can afford to go out either by themselves or in pairs. A further disadvantage is that in order to troll effectively the boat's engine must be kept running at all times. Even with inexpensive diesel fuel, this adds considerably to the cost of a day's fishing.

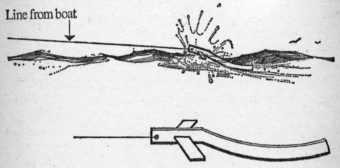

Line from boat

Detail of Shava-shava showing wings each side

Shava-shava

June 6th, 1970, was the day I caught my first porbeagle on a trolled bait and, to be honest, the whole thing happened quite accidentally after a long day's drifting for shark in the conventional manner. I had already caught a fish weighing 157 lb on float-fished mackerel, and was very pleased with my catch as it was the first shark of the year from the Isle of Wight grounds, opening up the new season in grand style. On this particular trip I was fishing from a private boat, the *Francis Bland*, and if it had not been for the fact that this boat was fitted with a direction finder, we would not have ventured out at all. Thick fog banks had blanketed the Channel, and the local forecast for St Catherine's area had given visibility as decreasing right through the day. The Solent was thick when we left Lymington, but visibility was reasonable at the Needles. After a brief stop to feather a couple of dozen bait-sized mackerel, we motored off down to St Catherine's. Here again visibility was passable, and so we picked up the first of the east-going tide, ran out our tackle, and began to drift right down the outside edge of St Catherine's deeps.

By two o'clock in the afternoon, we were still fishless and, as far as we could judge, some three miles off Dunose Point, east of Ventnor. The fog now began to thicken rapidly and by three o'clock it was difficult to keep track of the balloons in the swirling wastes that surrounded our boat. Ten minutes later, the 157-pounder picked up the bait, and fought it out for thirty minutes before coming reluctantly to the gaff. By this time the fog was really thick and we decided to stay put for the time being, in the hope it would eventually lift. Naturally enough, we continued to fish while we waited, but at 4.30, with no sign of the fog clearing, we decided to chance it and attempt to make our way back home to Lymington.

I always believe in taking one rod in at a time when shark fishing, just in case a fish comes on the scene at the last possible moment. On this day we had fished three rods, and with the other two sets of tackle safely inboard I started to retrieve my bait. Twenty feet away from the boat, I could see the mackerel wobbling along two or three feet below the surface. Then suddenly, right behind and below it, I saw a shark travelling at terrific speed, heading straight for the bait as it wobbled along. More by instinct than intention I threw my big Tatler reel out of gear as the shark struck. Sixty yards of line vanished in seconds, and then the fish spat out the mackerel. I waited for a minute or so to see if it would come back, but with no further sign of life at the other end of the line I began to reel in once again.

As the bait hit surface, a fin came up right behind it and for the second time the shark pounced on the moving mackerel. Again it tore off line, and again it dropped the bait, failing to return to it until I started to retrieve line. It struck twice more at the by now tattered mackerel, and each time it dropped it before I had a chance to set the hook. This particular shark was obviously only interested in a bait which moved: the moment the movement stopped it ejected the fish and ignored it. Naturally enough, we in the boat were in a high state of tension by the time the fish had picked up and dropped the bait for the fourth time. More in desperation than anything else, we decided to try to encourage the shark by trolling the bait away from it. Frankly, I was sure that the disturbance created by the engines would drive the obviously interested porbeagle away, but there seemed to be no other way of getting it to take the bait properly.

Even with the big engines just ticking over we seemed to me to be travelling far too fast for shark, but as the bait surfaced in our wake the fish came up once again. This time its dorsal fin and upper tail lobe protruded from the water as it took up position two or three yards behind the tatty remnants of my bait. I naturally had the rod in my hands, with my thumb ready to throw the reel out of gear the second the shark surged forward. Oddly enough, the fish seemed content just to follow the bait, and I suppose we must have travelled several hundred yards in this fashion before it finally made up its mind to nail the bait down. This time the attack was different. The shark seemed really intent on taking the bait rather than just playing about with it and, instead of rushing, it cruised up slowly, pushed its pointed snout out of the water and gulped in the remnants of the mackerel.

This time I had no doubt about hooking it, for I was absolutely certain that it had taken the bait right into its mouth. I did not even wait for the fish to stop and turn the bait, which just shows how confidently I assumed that it was mine for the taking. As I struck I felt the full weight of the shark against the rod tip, and as it went down I could feel that it was a reasonable fish, although not a really big one. Compared with the shark I had caught earlier in the day, this second fish put up a brilliant fight. I knew long before I saw it that my hook was lodged neatly in the corner of its heavy mouth. Lip-hooked shark always fight far better than throat- or gut-hooked fish, and one can usually tell just where a hook is placed by the overall reaction and speed of the fish during the time it is being played out.

When the shark finally rolled up alongside ready for the gaff, the hook showed clearly in the left-hand corner of its mouth. Shark hooked in this area of the jaw seldom manage to tear free and this one was no exception. Once we had heaved it inboard, it took a pair of heavy pliers and a very sharp knife to work the hook out of the muscle and gristle that separated the shark's upper and lower jaw. Somewhat smaller than the first fish, I estimated its weight at about 125 lb. Later on at the quay at Lymington, the scales registered the correct weight as 135 lb – not a very big shark by Isle of Wight standards, but a most interesting one by mine. Probably the first-ever Isle of Wight porbeagle caught on a trolled bait, it opened up a new field of angling and one upon which I am still working.

During the remainder of the 1970 season I caught several more shark on slowly trolled lures, and in each case the bait was a whole fresh mackerel. The next obvious step is to try to catch fish with artificial baits. If this is successful, it could mean that in future years shark anglers may discard the idea of using natural baits fished in a rubby-dubby slick, in favour of clean-to-handle, simple-to-obtain artificial baits. Many American shark fishermen have already made the switch from natural to artificial bait, without experiencing any loss of catches. Bob Reynolds and Fred Wagstaff, fishing from a small boat off the west coast of Ireland, had a big porbeagle snatch at a large plug bait and then escape, and according to the information I have received from America, plugs of one sort or another are regarded as the best type of artificial lure to use for shark.

American anglers believe that shark of all kinds have very

poor eyesight, and consequently that it is vibration and smell which helps them to home in on the bulk of their food. Because of this they tend to use artificial lures, which work rapidly and erratically as they are retrieved or trolled through the water. Surface plugs are their favourite lures, but I feel that in English waters, which are on average colder than those of America, deep-running plugs are more likely to succeed. Gurney-Grice of Christchurch gave me an immense yellow, plastic squid with a jointed body and huge soft plastic feelers to try out on porbeagles. This lure, designed originally for tuna fishing, measures over twelve inches in length and has obvious possibilities as a shark bait. Unfortunately, I have yet to have the opportunity of giving it a thorough testing.

Whether with an artificial or natural lure, trolling has immense possibilities as a sharking technique. It is a highly sporting method of fishing, and although as yet no really big shark have been caught on trolled lures, I can see no valid reason why a big fish will not sooner or later be struck in this way. Of the few fish I have had while trolling, each has been mouth hooked and each has put up a magnificent struggle. Thus, from the purely sport-fishing angle, this is a far superior way of catching shark. Although porbeagles are the most likely quarry for the trolling angler, makos will also strike at trolled natural baits and possibly artificial lures as well. Threshers are at best a totally unknown quantity and blues, according to anglers who have tried for them, ignore all trolled or spun baits – irrespective of whether they are natural or artificial. Anglers reading this section should, of course, keep an open mind on the comments I have made about blues and threshers, simply because as yet we know so little about their overall reactions to trolled lures.

Very little has been achieved in this particular field of angling, and when anglers state definitely that a particular type of shark will not under any circumstances strike at a particular type of bait, they usually base their whole opinion on the results of a few hours non-productive angling when the shark were probably in a non-responsive mood anyway. I believe that any angler who is willing to go out, day after day, trolling for shark would find that all types of shark, whether they be blue, thresher, porbeagle or mako, would at some time or another succumb to his bait. Only time and constant fishing can prove this conclusively. We already know that all these shark are active predators, catching the bulk of their food alive, and thus one can fairly safely assume that they will all give chase to a moving bait which either simulates the movement of a normal fish, or gives off vibrations which they find attractive.

The Americans have taken the business of sport fishing for shark very much to heart, with the result that they deliberately spin for shark, and often with spectacular results. Fly fishing for shark is another up and coming method much practised by American anglers. This is usually a shallow-water technique, and the anglers use specially constructed salt-water fly rods, reels and lines for the job. A favourite technique of the Americans is to use rubby-dubby, locally called 'chum', to attract the shark close to the boat; the moment the fish put in an appearance, out comes the fly or spinning rod and in comes the shark. If we ever get to the stage of using this tackle for British sharks, most anglers will have the added pleasure of constructing their own flies and lures. There is enormous scope for this kind of bait making, and even the most ham-fisted angler should be able to design lures suitable for sharking. Personally, I hope we do get to this stage, for it will add to the enormous pleasure of shark hunting, and open new fields for us to explore and exploit.

Finishing Them Off

Once a shark is secured alongside a boat with its tail drawn right up out of the water, it can either be left to drown or it can be heaved right inboard and finished off quickly and humanely in the boat. I am personally in favour of killing the fish as quickly as possible, firstly to avoid unnecessary cruelty to the creature and secondly because any live shark, no matter how tired it may be, is potentially a very dangerous customer to have hanging about either inside or outside a boat. Even a small shark can inflict a very nasty wound with its teeth, and a big one snapping wildly at anything within reach can be a really ugly brute to deal with.

Oddly enough, although all sharks have enormous reserves of strength, they can be killed quickly by hitting them hard on the nose. I use a wooden mallet for this job and normally find one or two hard blows with this instrument are more than enough to send the shark to sleep. One should never assume that any shark is completely dead, however. I have known fish which have apparently expired to lunge forward suddenly, snapping wildly at all and sundry. These spasms are normally caused by nerve reflexes, but even though the fish is practically dead and obviously cannot exert too much pressure with its jaws, it can still cause serious damage should it latch on to a foot or a leg.

Shark to Order

Shark fishing is an exciting, hard-hitting sport and as such it interests the general public far more than any other form of angling. Because of its obvious appeal, I often get requests from newspapers and television companies to take out reporters or camera crews, so that they can write or film sharking for public consumption. Catching fish to order in this way can be a nerve-racking experience, for shark of any size are nomadic wanderers which shift from one locality to another according to tide or weather changes. This is bad enough when you are trying to find fish for a normal angling party, but when your party consists of two cameramen, a sound-man and a director, all of whom know nothing about shark fishing or for that matter the sea life, it can become very difficult indeed; particularly when the TV or newspaper crew expect instant action, so that they can finish their job as quickly as possible and get back ashore for a good long session in one of the local pubs.

One of the first 'shark to order' jobs I ever did was for Southern Television for the 'Day by Day' programme. The idea was to shoot enough usable film to make a ten-minute colour feature which would then be scheduled for showing during the evening peak-viewing period. Obviously, the whole operation had to be planned very carefully, paying strict attention to all the minute details which if omitted could ruin a film of this kind. Finally, after a week of lengthy telephone calls and innumerable changes of plan, the great day dawned and we all gathered on the quay at Lymington ready for the off. Even a small camera team carries an unbelievable amount of luggage, and by the time all the boxes of film stock, spare camera, bodies, lenses, tripods, lunch bags, etc had been loaded aboard, there was very little space to spare for a fish, should we be lucky enough to catch one.

By my reckoning, the day was far too good too early and the bright sunshine and lack of any sort of breeze made me suspicious of the day ahead. Through bitter experience I have learned to read all the signs of bad weather around the Island and I could feel that this was one of those days which promises a great deal to start with, and then changes incredibly rapidly. At the Needles, 'the bridge' was flatter than I have ever seen it, and away to the west 'Old Harry' rocks shone brilliant white in the morning sun. Even with a sea like glass, mackerel were comparatively scarce – yet another sign that the weather was on the change for worse. The St Catherine's overfall area was absolutely calm when we arrived, and as we ran out the shark lines, tested the reels, and posed for the preliminary baiting-up shots, I wondered just how much time we would have before the day turned sour on us.

With the tide in our favour and a good rubby-dubby slick spilling out behind us, a fair shoal of mackerel put in a surprise appearance and for a while the television men abandoned their equipment in favour of handlines furnished with mackerel feathers. As leash after leash of prime big mackerel came out of the glassy water, I was lulled into believing that possibly my instincts had misled me, and that in fact this would be one of those rare flat days which occasionally occur off the Island. The strong spring tide under our keel and the lack of any restraining wind enabled our boat to drift east at quite a fair speed, and I began to feel more and more content with the day and the fishing I hoped it would bring.

Then, from the south-west, came the faintest suggestion of a breeze; nothing more than a gentle whisper that barely ruffled the surface. This and the tide working together pushed us along a little faster, and as St Catherine's Lighthouse passed behind us I had the feeling that already shark were with us. I can never explain just how or why I know when a shark starts to trail the boat I am fishing from, but know I do, and more often than not I am right about my hunch. By this time the breeze had begun to pick up considerably, and as the surface water turned into small short waves, tiny white horses began to show on the surface.

Thirty minutes later, almost directly off Ventnor, one of our balloon floats registered a short bite, then nothing. A bait inspection showed a clean hook, and so, deciding to take no chances, I checked the bait on the second rod. This time the bait had been neatly chopped off at both ends, leaving a well-chewed lump of fish adhering to the bend of the big hook. Obviously the shark, or more likely the sharks whose presence I had sensed earlier, had swum along with us, munching at the baits without making any attempt to take them properly. Small shark are often responsible for this sort of bait mutilation, and although I hoped for a really big fish I was happy enough to accept a medium-sized one early on in the day, so that at least the TV team would be able to put something on film to start them off. Pulling both sets of gear in for rebaiting takes a few minutes and it was not until I started to run out the baits for the second time that I realized just how strong the wind had become. Force 5–7 was my reckoning and already a really ugly big sea was beginning to build up round us.

Within five minutes, one of the camera team and the reporter/producer were hanging head down over the side and the second cameraman looked as though he would join them at the slightest excuse. On this particular day I had Graham Allen of Liss out with me as second angler. The enormous swell was making the boat buck like a mad horse, and we both realized that our only hope of a shark was to hold the rod and feel for a biting fish, since it was obvious that we would never see the balloon float move in the heavy sea and flying spray. I have seen the Isle of Wight shark grounds in all their moods, but never have I seen them change as suddenly as they did on this particular day. To veer from a flat calm to a truly raging sea in less than an hour seems almost unbelievable, but that is how it went.

Now, to make matters even worse, Graham's rod tip nodded twice very heavily, and we knew for certain that once again a shark had found his bait, even in that maelstrom of water. The second cameraman was still on his feet and, grasping what was happening, he swung the big heavy camera into position and made ready to film. Graham's rod twitched heavily again, and then sprang back as he released slack line to the pulling fish. His intention had been to give the shark just a yard or two of slack to play with, but it had other ideas and the twitching bites turned into a full-blooded run as the fish engulfed the mackerel and took off. By this stage all of us aboard realized that the sooner we got under way and steamed off home, the better off we would be.

This was obviously no time for taking the finer points of angling into account and Graham, who knows his shark fishing as well as anyone, did not mess about with his fish. From the moment he set the hook, he rough-housed the shark as much as possible and at times he put more pressure on his tackle than he should have done. From the rapidly weakening cameraman's point of view, this was just what was wanted. The fish was taking terrific stick and the rod was bent over at an acute angle which would obviously look well on film. In the filthy sea conditions, both angler and fish took a terrible physical thrashing and at one time it was touch and go who would give in first.

Fortunately, by Island standards, this was only a small shark and so Graham came out the winner – although when the fish first saw the boat it made several determined attempts to break free. It even jumped clear out of the water in full view of the camera. This was almost certainly a unique opportunity for the television company, since porbeagle shark seldom make any attempt to jump, even when they are hooked. Within minutes of the fish breaching, I had the gaff into it, and as it came snapping over the side and fell into the well of the boat, the camera-man flopped over, too sick even to finish off the film.

This was the very first shark-fishing film made on the Isle of Wight grounds and its subsequent showing on Southern Television's network helped to spread the word that the Island shark grounds were opened up and available for fishing. Constant bad weather made this particular day difficult from a filming point of view, but even in totally adverse conditions I managed to find a shark for the camera crew to film and in this respect the whole outing was a total success. The television team paid heavily in terms of sheer physical discomfort but they stood it well and, like true professionals, came home with a good feature film.

In July 1971, the BBC came to me with a similar request, this time to make a shark and a conger film on the same day, the idea being to fit both into an angling series which they intended showing at peak-viewing times. Two films in one day is a pretty tall order, and the shark film was obviously going to be the most difficult of the two. We made an early start from Lymington in the hope that we would arrive on the shark grounds in time to finish the film early, so that we could go on to the conger mark as soon as possible. Jonathan Webb was to be the 'star' of the film, although the idea was for us to put out a rod apiece, so that we stood twice the chance of hooking a fish.

Weather is always our main worry, as the waters around the Isle of Wight are notorious for their tide races and overfall areas, which whip up at the first indication of wind. This time we were obviously going to be lucky. It was one of those rare days off the Island when the wind was non-existent and the St Catherine's overfall area was as flat as a pancake. Mackerel, which had been scarce, appeared in vast numbers that day and within minutes of stopping the boat and lowering the rubby-dubby bag over the side, I had a bucketful of fresh bait-sized fish inboard. Fresh baits are absolutely essential for shark fishing and with the mackerel shoaling in millions, I could already sense the presence of shark in the area round the boat. Neap tides and total lack of wind made drifting difficult but the slight east-going tide carried us slowly along.

I could see that our rubby-dubby slick was sinking down instead of flowing directly away from the boat, and taking this point into consideration, it seemed to me that a deep-set bait would in all probability attract a shark. Normally most of the porbeagles we catch fall to baits presented at depths of thirty feet or less, and it was at this depth that Jonathan elected to fish his bait. My own tackle was set at just under fifty feet. As I baited up with two mackerel and slid my bait over the side into the calm water, I felt absolutely one-hundred per cent confident that I would get a fish. Sure enough, after drifting for about forty minutes, my balloon float dipped sharply, bobbed up and down twice, then turned in a big circle and came hurtling back towards the boat at tremendous speed, leaving me to wind the reel handle like a maniac in an attempt to pick up the slack line created by the fish.

These tearaway bites always worry me, for it is impossible to judge accurately just when to hit a fish which obviously has no immediate intention of stopping to turn the bait in its jaws. This fish gave a typical example of the kind of bite I mean. As it approached the boat, it seemed to pick up speed, the balloon gradually submerging as it came closer. At the last possible moment it veered away, clearing the stern by less than a yard. As it sped past I just sat back and waited for the slack line to come tight. When this happened, I struck the hook firmly home, reeled in the resulting slack line and struck twice more for good measure. This particular shark did not take long to realize that it was in trouble and, unlike most fish which are sluggish to start with, this chap shifted into top gear the second I sank the hook, and took off like a race horse.

The camera team were already filming and I could see that

my rod had an impressive battle curve in it, which was exactly what was required for the film. A big fish fighting hard on a very hot day can be a real handful, and by the end of the first fifteen minutes of the battle the sweat was pouring off me in streams. Shortly after this, however, the shark began to weaken noticeably, and it was not over-long before I was able to fight it to the surface. Long before I could see the fish I knew it was not a big one. I guessed it was somewhere between 130–150 lb, and as it surfaced I could see that I was not going to be far out in this assessment.

In the gin-clear water, every detail stood out sharply and I immediately noticed that it had a strangely shaped dorsal fin. Normally, a shark's dorsal is a clear-cut triangular pennant, standing high and stiff. This fish had an oddly curled dorsal which gave it a lop-sided look in the water. It is curious just how much can be seen in the split second it takes a big fish to pass astern of a boat, and this one crossed back and forth twice more, directly below the transom of the boat. Then, all of a sudden, it hit surface with a rush and beat the water to foam with its broad scythe-like tail. The effort of this mad flurry weakened it considerably, and without too much trouble I was able to hold it near to the surface so that the camera-man could film it at close range.

At this stage the film ran out and the producer calmly asked me to keep the fish hanging about while a fresh magazine was being fitted to the camera. Even a tired, well-beaten shark cannot be horsed about for long on the surface, and so I played safe and eased up on the reel drag, allowing the fish to run out line while the cameraman fiddled about with his toys. I would say that ten minutes elapsed before everything was ready to roll again. By this time, the fish had managed to get its second wind and was in the process of sounding – with the obvious intention of hitting bottom and staying there. This made life difficult for me, since in order to continue shooting the film in sequence it was essential to get the fish back on surface as near to its original position as possible. In all, it took me ten minutes of hard pumping to lift it yard by yard back towards the surface, but finally it came up in exactly the right area and rolled over to expose its white belly to the camera.

With the surface action shots securely in the can, it was simply a matter of moments to bring the fish into gaffing range. While the skipper grasped the heavy wire trace in both hands, I laid down the rod, picked up the big flying gaff and drove it hard into the fish's belly. Seconds later the tailer was slipped over its feebly wagging tail, and with a quick heave the shark was out of the water and into the boat before it had time even to attempt any form of violent protest against gaff and tail wire. The film was later shown on the BBC's 'South Today' programme, and although as an angler I could see some faults in its presentation, it attracted a lot of interest and added a little more to the reputation of the Isle of Wight shark grounds.

If you have enjoyed this PAN
Book, you may like to choose
your next book from the titles
listed on the following pages.

Anglers' Library

BOAT FISHING
Trevor Housby   40p

Describes the most productive boat fishing
techniques for saltwater species. Sea fishing is
increasingly popular and many new types of
tackle have been devised to catch more and
larger fish. They are all described here, together with a wealth of practical hints and
methods used by the author, who runs a mod-
ern Sea Angling Centre at Lymington which
is often featured on TV.

'Bang up-to-date with ideas ... Exceptionally
good value for money' – BBC

'Practical, down-to-earth approach' – SCOTSMAN

Anglers' Library

COARSE FISHING
Edited by Kenneth Mansfield   40p

Seven authors, each well known for their writing on angling topics, provide the complete hand-book on coarse fishing for every angler. All the main species are dealt with individually, together with full descriptions of tackle and techniques. Baits – how to find, clean and use them – are covered in the same comprehensive manner and there is a wealth of other useful information.

'Very good value' – EASTERN DAILY EXPRESS

Anglers' Library

CANAL FISHING
Kenneth Seaman   35p

The author deals with this increasingly popular sport in a helpful, lucid manner. Traditional methods and tackles are critically examined together with advice on bait selection and preparation. There are chapters on angling for all the well-known species as well as the more unusual chubb, dace and rudd. Match fishing techniques are fully discussed, a fresh approach to ground baiting suggested and the problems of canal maintenance highlighted.

'Practical, down-to-earth approach' – SCOTSMAN

'An admirable series' – DAILY TELEGRAPH

These and other PAN Books are obtainable from all booksellers and newsagents. If you have any difficulty please send purchase price plus 7p postage to PO Box 11, Falmouth, Cornwall.
While every effort is made to keep prices low, it is sometimes necessary to increase prices at short notice. PAN Books reserve the right to show new retail prices on covers which may differ from those advertised in the text or elsewhere.